To Rabbi Max Shapiro:

With gratitude —

Jacob Neusner

Abraham J. Peck

Studies in the
American Jewish Experience

Edited by
Jacob R. Marcus
and
Abraham J. Peck

The American Jewish Archives

Studies in the American Jewish Experience

Contributions from the Fellowship Programs of the American Jewish Archives

Volume I

American Jewish Archives
On the Cincinnati Campus of the
Hebrew Union College-Jewish Institute of Religion

Copyright © 1981
American Jewish Archives

Library of Congress Cataloging in Publication Data

Studies in the American Jewish experience.

Includes bibliographical references and index.
1. Jews — United States — History — Addresses, essays, lectures. 2. United States — Ethnic relations — Addresses, essays, lectures. I Marcus, Jacob Rader, 1896-
II. Peck, Abraham J. III. American Jewish Archives.
E184.J5S872   973'.04924   81-1294
ISBN 0-87820-010-X   AACR2

Manufactured in the United States of America

*This volume is dedicated to
Professor Alfred Gottschalk
on the occasion of his tenth year as
president of the Hebrew Union
College-Jewish Institute of Religion
and for his devotion to the
history of the American Jewish experience*

Table of Contents

		Page
Preface	JACOB R. MARCUS ABRAHAM J. PECK	7
Elliot Cohen: The Vocation of a Jewish Literary Mentor	ELINOR GRUMET	8
From Russia to America: Baruch Charney Vladeck and the Evolution of Jewish Socialism	FRANKLIN JONAS	26
A Decade of Promise: General Eisenhower, European and American Jewry, and Israel, 1942-1952	IAN J. BICKERTON	46
"Touch Life and You Will Find It Good": Charles Wessolowsky and the Southern Jewish Experience	LOUIS SCHMIER	64
Immigrant Jewish Women in Los Angeles: Occupation, Family and Culture	NORMA FAIN PRATT	78
Francis E. Abbot: Perceptions of a Nineteenth Century Religious Radical on Jews and Judaism	BENNY KRAUT	90
Contributors		114
American Jewish Archives Fellowship Programs		115
Fellows of the American Jewish Archives, 1977-1981		116
Index		118

Preface

In 1977 the American Jewish Archives initiated its Fellowship Programs. Since that time nearly two dozen scholars, both doctoral and post-doctoral, have been appointed Fellows under one or more of our programs. A number of these Fellows, have come from universities outside of the United States, a positive sign that scientific research in the American Jewish experience is beginning to interest serious scholars on an international level.

The need for such Fellowship programs had been evident to the American Jewish Archives for a number of years. American Jewish history, indeed American Jewish studies in general, is a relatively new discipline, still very much a developing one in terms of theory and methodology. A meeting place which would allow the most fertile minds working in the discipline to gather and exchange views on different aspects of the field (while researching their own projects) was a clear *desideratum*.

But where to start? The first step was obviously financial. We were certainly aware of the travel and subsistence costs of doing extensive research, both to financially hard-pressed graduate students and faculty. Fortunately, a most generous and cultured group of patrons answered our needs by establishing the Fellowship programs now offered by our institution. To these patrons we are eternally grateful. We hope that potential patrons, also eager to support the development of American Jewish history, will help to further our programs.

During the past two summers, 1979 and 1980, the American Jewish Archives has sponsored a number of research seminars in which our post-doctoral Fellows have presented their research findings in seminar form before a distinguished group of faculty members from the Hebrew Union College-Jewish Institute of Religion and its neighboring institution, the University of Cincinnati. The sessions have been intellectually exciting and most fruitful, both to the audience of assembled scholars and to those presenting their research. We have no doubts that the insights developed from those stimulating seminars are reflected in the following contributions.

Jacob R. Marcus, Director
American Jewish Archives

Abraham J. Peck, Associate Director
American Jewish Archives

Elliot Cohen:
The Vocation of a
Jewish Literary Mentor

Elinor Grumet

Elliot Cohen
(1899-1959)
Courtesy of the American Jewish Committee, New York

"Little magazines" — which, if financially stable, lose their diminutive epithet but not their function — are the places where American intellectuals have met one another since early in the century. The criticism sometimes levelled against groups of intellectuals, that they mostly read one another, is more useful as a sociological insight than as a response to any given set of ideas. For intellectual magazines have made loose communities out of otherwise isolated individuals. Like cafes or ale houses, intellectual magazines give a writer a place to talk, and ongoing conversations in which to participate. Beyond camaraderie and occasion, a writer may also find in such magazines the stimulus of authoritative style, of a craftsmanship that is effective.

In the group that has come to be called the New York Jewish intelligentsia, two magazines figure significantly, especially for conversations on Jewish matters of interest: the *Menorah Journal*, which last appeared in 1962, and *Commentary* magazine, still being published. Both, in formative periods, were dominated by the editorship of Elliot Cohen – the *Menorah Journal* from 1924 to 1931, and *Commentary* from its inception in 1945 to Cohen's illness and death in the late 1950s. Elliot Cohen, more than any other individual of his time, encouraged and maintained a community of secular Jewish discourse in English from which writers of two generations made their way.

Elliot Cohen – named by his mother after George Eliot (she surely had in mind the writer's sympathetic exposition of Jewish "racial" and national sentiment in Daniel Deronda) – was born into a family of spirited but unorthodox Jewish commitment, in either Des Moines or nearby Tama, Iowa, on March 15, 1899. Cohen family imagination has dwelled especially on Ellot's maternal grandfather, Samuel Aaron Ettelson, as the beloved and salty patriarch of the group, and most of the five Cohen children took Ettelson as their middle name. Samuel was a *maskil* from Lithuania who first found his way to Texarkana, Texas. Eventually he settled in Mobile when his train to New York stopped there, and he was taken with the city. Mobile was then a leisurely-paced port; few streets were paved or well-lit, but its high society was only second to New Orlean's. Ettelson had been a Hebrew teacher in Europe. In America he became a jeweller, who published both prose and verse in various Hebrew and Yiddish periodicals in this country. Avocationally he used to write letters to the newspapers, seek out strangers in crowds, and from his porch hail friends for conversation. He tolerated religious observance in his wife until he thought it excessive; then – according to family legend – he smeared her dishes with lard. He would go to the Reform temple but leave noisily with his cane at the sermon; and he admonished his youngest granddaughter to resent Zionism, because of the position of women in biblical society. Still true to the Enlightenment, in 1923, at the age of 72, he published an autobiographical novel and poetry (including a sonnet on Babe Ruth) in classical Hebrew, in Prague. Both Elliott and his brother Mandel hoped to write a book about him.[1]

Samuel Ettelson's daughter Rosa, a fancy dressmaker, left for Chicago to look for a husband, there being few eligible Jewish men in Mobile; her three sisters who remained behind never married. In Chicago, at the home of a cousin, she met Harry Cohen, a young peddler from Iowa who came periodically to the big city to buy goods and look for a wife. Cohen (the family name had previously been Gabalsky), was born in 1870 in Sewalki, Russian Poland, and had been a student at the Volozhin Yeshiva, continuing his studies there even after his family had emigrated to the

American midwest. Only the threat of conscription in the army of the Czar caused him to repeat their odyssey and abandon his studies before he was ordained. Although Elliot Cohen's father did not choose to be an American rabbi, he acted unofficially as adjudicant for all religious disputes and questions in Mobile; he was the president of the Orthodox congregation, and advised the Reform group, of which he was also a member; he was deeply involved in the community, an active Zionist, working for European relief during the first World War. But his religious observance was too attenuated to offset the influence of his waggish father-in-law. He raised his children on kosher meat but one set of dishes; studied Jewish texts after hours, but did business on Saturdays; held a Seder at Passover, but "skipped a lot." The Bible, he taught, was to be understood only as allegory and legend. This pragmatic, adjusted observance had the effect of secularizing his family, while giving them a strong cultural feel for Judaism.[2]

Elliot later said that his family history was the typical immigrant story, but he forgot the southern landscape—for the man who was to confirm the literary and personal style of New York Jewish intellectuals was raised in Alabama. The peddler and his wife bore their first son while still struggling in Iowa. When the boy was five or six, they had been sufficiently successful to contemplate opening a store, and moved to her home in Mobile to do so. The Cohens opened a dry goods business, selling clothing and notions on the main street in the black section of town. The clientele was mixed—blacks, poor whites, Jews, hillbillies, a few of the more prosperous townspeople; with all of them relations were comfortable. They lived over the store, and their location was the occasional cause of the children's being taunted at the white school. Later, when he became prosperous, Harry Cohen moved his family to the best street in the city; but the apartment on Davis Avenue was Elliot's home until he left for Yale at the age of fifteen.[3]

Harry Cohen from Sewalki came to look the Southern colonel—short, dignified, he wore a black suit and starched collar, so that Cohen's bride Sylvia thought he might have been born on a plantation. He had a strong personality, was impressive and brilliantly witty; and Rose was quick, emotional, "un-rebettsin-like." The family, which extended to include the maiden aunts, was voluble—a tableful of talkers served for thirty-five years by a Creole cook who learned to make jambolaya with *gribenes* instead of shrimp.[4]

Apparently the children were greatly pressed to achieve; there are family legends of young Elliot's brilliance—his reading labels on cans, and expressing the desire to be a writer at a startlingly early age. "I knew I wanted to be a writer when I was six," Cohen said in an interview, and linked his early longing for books to that passionate preoccupation of his family which had given him his name. Perhaps what his brother Mandel wrote in a review of a Jewish children's book in the *Menorah Journal* tells us something about his own upbringing:

> Abie (the hero of the book) is primarily a brain-worker and his uniform success is likely to encourage that much deplored predilection of the Jew for intellectual pursuits. Abie makes brain-work look too easy, and that is likely to prove more dangerous to Bernard's future than all fifteen volumes of Jack Harkavy. Little Bernard (the prototypical Jewish son) realizes when he reads the Jack Harkavy books that Jack really couldn't, in reason, win so many fights. Little Bernie has been in fights himself and has been consistently bashed. After one good sock in the eye at seven he is not likely to set his heart on being a noble man of iron fists. But, the brain being more firmly encased than the eye, Bernard will never feel the impact of intellectual defeats in the same immediate way. He will believe implicitly in wits like Abie's, and will come to believe in the potency of the wits of little Bernard. He will believe at college, with a hundred thousand other Bernards, that he is destined to be a writer, he will graduate knowing that he is a critic, and do post-graduate work convinced that he is a wit. Nor will he ever—even twenty years after, when he has doubled papa's pants business—be reconciled to not being a second Bernard Shaw or at least a second Christopher Morley. A hundred thousand Jewish tragedies lurk within the covers of this innocent-seeming book.[5]

Mandel, on Elliot's encouragement, exchanged his dreams of writing for psychiatry. The older brother was a powerful presence in the lives of his siblings, and on their part there was equal acquiescence and resentment of the authority which he claimed.[6]

Although Elliot Cohen told Henry Hurwitz, the founder of the journal, that he had other offers, the *Menorah* apprenticeship may have been the first offer of work Cohen had after spending four undergraduate years at Yale, and five in its graduate school in the Department of English. His career there was characterized by brilliance and a failure of academic heart or will. Cohen was fairly withdrawn from college activities. He was industrious, a "grind." As a graduate student, he could most often be found reading in the English Seminar Room at the top of the stairs in Lynsly-Chittendon Hall; and he was well-read on all matters of contemporary literature. But he could not finish his graduate degree: He had planned to expand a seminar paper on the sixteenth-century playwright James Shirley into a Ph.D. dissertation. But after five years, even the Masters was not awarded him because he had neither completed his language requirements nor submitted a Master's thesis. And his professor, Tucker Brooke, barely passed him, noting on his record: "Clever but lazy. Work quite good occasionally but lacking earnestness and consistency." Other teachers were impressed by his quickness: Cohen was graduated Phi Beta Kappa, the youngest in the class of 1918, and was awarded Yale's John Addison Porter Fellowship for two years of graduate work in English.

In a note to the dean in 1921, Chauncy Tinker expressed the feeling that Cohen's record did not entitle him to any special consideration from the department. Later Cohen spoke of Tinker's anti-Semitism. Now there lay a reason for Cohen's resistance to academic study deeper than the literary radicalism Randolph Bourne had felt several years earlier, and compounded with it. Being Jewish and named Cohen, Elliot had no hope of a teaching appointment in a university department of English. His fate would be Horace Kallen's at Princeton or Ludwig Lewisohn's at Columbia: He would be dismissed or not accepted at all. A close gentile friend of Cohen's at this time, a classmate, remembers that "most doors were closed to Elliot, or he thought they were."[7]

The only professional connection Cohen apparently maintained from these years was with the Luce empire. He was greatly admired there, and, according to Louis Berg, sometimes sat in on policy meetings. But his campus literary life was not public, not lived in the official organizations. He is not remembered in Yale's official history, and even in 1918, his name does not appear among the many in his class that ebullient professor of English William Lyon Phelps says he will miss. Needless to say, he was not invited to join the exclusive Elizabethan Club. While at Yale, Cohen's affiliations were those of identity and not literature: He belonged only to the Southern Club (being from Mobile, Alabama), and the Menorah Society. His Menorah Prize Essay on "the promise of the American Synagogue" published in the *Menorah Journal* in 1918, is apparently Cohen's only student publication.[8]

By 1927, Elliot Cohen had established the literary reputation of the *Menorah Journal*, putting it in a class with magazines like the *Dial* and the *American Mercury*. In that year, Henry Hurwitz, the *Menorah's* editor-in-chief, then preoccupied with keeping the Menorah enterprise financially solvent, moved the office of the organization to its third location . . . in Manhattan—on the outskirts of Greenwich Village, at the northeast corner of Fifth Avenue and Thirteenth Street in one of the old mansions that used to line Fifth Avenue, at number 63. Here Cohen filled the suite of rooms with the traffic of young writers of various intensities, who wrote for him and came to seek his encouragement and advice. Cohen's office had been the hall bedroom of the house. He had the habit of watching people in the street from the large window and commenting on their lives; he wrote his correspondence out longhand for his secretary with small, scrubby pencils. Most of the young people who wrote for the *Menorah Journal* were likely to feel, as Lionel Trilling did, that Henry Hurwitz was "a man with whom it was impossible to converse, at least if you were young and clever. He was shy and stiff, without wit and with no more than a formal humor, and he easily became defensive. . . ." It was for Cohen the young men wrote.[9]

During this period, most of those involved with the *Menorah* lived in the Village, though Lionel Trilling moved there only in 1929. (Hurwitz was the major exception; he lived with his family in the gracious suburb of Larchmont.) The Village then was a lively, literary neighborhood—the legendary Village. The offices of the *Dial*, the *Liberator*, and *Broom* were short walks away; and in the late 20s Marianne Moore, Elinor Wylie and William Rose Benet, Sinclair Lewis and Dorothy Thompson, Thomas Wolfe, e. e. cummings, Meyer Schapiro, and Allen Tate, among others, called the Village home. The lower East Side was a few blocks east, and Cohen and some of the *Journal* writers frequented the Cafe Royale, a haunt of the Yiddish-speaking literati.[10]

Edward Dahlberg drifted in and out of the office, expounding his views of life and the novelist Irving Fineman published in the *Menorah Journal* during this period and was there quite a bit. Maxwell Bodenheim came in with "green hair and absolutely nuts." Albert Halper and Kenneth Fearing brought their work to the office, a little disheveled from poverty. Cohen had a magnetic quality; he drew young writers to him and exacted from them the best literary work of which they were capable, coaxing them to confront their Jewish experience for material. Twenty years later as editor of *Commentary*, Cohen was still teaching his writers, Norman Podhoretz remembers, that "things Jewish could be talked about with the same disinterestedness, the same candor, the same range of reference, and the same resonance as any serious subject." Cohen, in fact, shared Hurwitz's zeal for winning bright young (and not-so-young) men back to the fold. Having convinced Irwin Edman, Professor of Philosophy at Columbia, to write a series of articles for the journal, Cohen wrote Hurwitz:

> ... this is one more scalp for us. The Salvation Army are not the only people on the block who scrag people back to Jesus. Maybe we should have a revival meeting of the Menorah Mission someday and have testimonials from all the returned saved. ..[11]

And Edman himself wrote Hurwitz: "I did not know when I started that the *Journal* was going to make a good Jew of me." "You ought to have heard me at eigtheen." Recalling his own situation, Loius Berg said that the writers' wives often resented Cohen—less for the male-bonding of the group he formed around him, than for keeping the men involved in Jewish work, where they couldn't earn a living.[12]

Only a few years older than those whose talents he developed, Cohen assumed the role of father and mentor. "He never played the game of being young," Trilling recalled. "He entranced and infuriated us." Talk was his charm. Cohen's secretary brought to the office her old friend Felix Morrow (ne Mayrowitz), then a junior at NYU. "In a really Svengali-fashion," Morrow recalls, "he enticed me into a series of discussions out of which emerged his persuading me to write that first thing I wrote—that history of Brownsville." Cohen held Albert Halper in conversation for two hours after the *Journal* had just bought its first story from him, drawing him out until the young writer, who was living in isolation, worried that he was talking too much. Trilling observed that Cohen was a "Socratic personality, drawing young men to him to be teased and taught. He conversed endlessly, his talk being a sort of enormously enlightening gossip-about persons, books, baseball players and football plays, manners, morals, comedians (on these he was especially good), clergyman (with an emphasis on rabbis, one of whom he once described as 'the Jewish Stephen Wise'), colleges, the social sciences, philanthropy and social work, literary scholarship, restaurants, tailors, psychiatry." Cohen was a speculative talker and thinker, with a teacher's intention: grasping the point of an issue, he played until he had made his interlocutor think of it and value his part in the game.[13]

Clifton Fadiman, like Herbert Solow, was a friend of Trilling's who was brought into the *Menorah* circle by him. Albert Halper tells the story that years later, Fadiman would clap his hand on Cohen's back at parties and introduce him as the man who'd taught him how to write. Many felt the same way. Cohen assumed a protective relationship to those he considered his writers, driving them himself to revise their work and revise it again, carefully explaining each time what was wrong. "No one," wrote Trilling, "—certainly none of our teachers—ever paid so much attention to what we thought and how we wrote." Cohen inspired those around him with a sense of their own importance and elicited their best work. Trilling recalled that he had come to the *Journal* intent upon developing an embellished, "literary," style, and learned simplicity from Cohen. After Cohen's extended depression and suicide in 1959, his funeral was attended by scores of people whose talents he had brought out. Cohen's way with both new and more secure writers was aggressive and affectionate. That first interview of Halper's (who regards Cohen as his "literary godfather") was initiated by the editor, and concluded with an invitation to his home for dinner. Cohen took special pains with the writing of non-English speakers. Later, as editor of *Commentary*, he labored over Hannah Arendt's essays; in the 1920s he sent Herbert Solow to work on Salo Baron's English at his office at the Jewish Institute of Religion. Meyer Levin, an undergraduate at the Universty of Chicago was contacted by Cohen after an editorial canvas of Jewish talent in university literary magazines, and so Levin's first story in a major periodical appeared in the *Menorah Journal*. Cohen lent Albert Halper money and recommended him to Yaddo as a serious writer. Charles Reznikoff was first compensated for his work in the pages of the *Menorah Journal* under Cohen; in the 1950s, Cohen helped Reznikoff receive the commission to edit the letters of Louis Marshall.[14]

Cohen' innovations on the *Menorah Journal* were several: First, he initiated a section called "Commentaries," which encouraged the compostion of "Material of a brief, informal, and personal nature" and short pieces of fiction about Jewish life in the spirit of local color. (When Norman Podhoretz inherited the editorship of *Commentary* magazine in 1960, he found incomprehesible Cohen's readiness to publish fiction of a "distressingly vulgar coziness." The *Commentary* stories "From the American Scene" were remnants of Cohen's earlier effort to create a native American-Jewish literature.) Louis Berg was one of the most frequent contributors to this section; he also worked with Cohen in 1930 and 1931 as associate editor of the *Journal,* although Hurwitz would not permit his name to appear on the letterhead because Berg was not college-educated. Berg had first seen the *Menorah Journal* in the hands of an eccentric uncle while working as a stevedore on the railroads in Virginia, where he was raised after being brought to America from Kovno. He felt a "shock of surprise" that there should be such a Jewish literary magazine, and sent off a story he had written. After Berg moved to New York, Cohen made use of his bread-and-butter Yiddish—more Yiddish than anyone else on the staff commanded—to translate the work of David Bergelson. Altogether, Berg sold eighteen light stories to the *Menorah Journal* as "Commentaries"—for example, about a Jewish boy in a Southern town, whose gift for cursing wins the Jews' acceptance there; about an old woman who takes a young husband; about a grocer who is magnificently duped. During this period Berg supported himself as a reporter on the Brownsville *News* and the New York *Journal*.[15]

Then Cohen encouraged the investigative reporting of Jewish communal affairs and events of Jewish interest in a section called "Chronicles," initiated in 1928. Such journalism was an enormous advance in the English-language Jewish press; a footnote was sometimes used to assure the reader that the article was "factual even down to the names of persons and places." These pieces combine a lively subjectivity with appropriate research, and are among the greatest fruits of the *Menorah Journal's* independence. Again Berg was a significant contributor. The "Chronicles" section contains, for example, reports on a Conference of the Joint Distribution Committee; the Convention of the Zionist Organization of America of 1928; reviews of the American and Palestinian press after the 1929 riots in Palestine; a report on anti-Semitic violence in Romania written by someone just returned; a description of the "class struggle" between Jewish workers and landowners in Petach Tikvah; a report written in 1931 on the collapse of the boom in Jewish philanthropy; an assessment of the Biro-Bidzhan proposal; a memoir and expose of the Jewish Legion, organized under Jabotinsky in World War I, written by one who had served in it; a discussion of the gangsterism and politics controlling the kosher chicken market in New York City; and a report on the court battles to open to Jews the exclusive Sea Gates area of Brooklyn.[16]

In this spirit, Cohen encouraged the political reporting of Herbert Solow, another associate editor—a graduate of Columbia, then on the editorial satff of the *Encyclopedia of the Social Sciences,* and later an editor of *Fortune* magazine. Solow's hot temper and his articles critical of Zionism aggravated the relationship of the young intellectuals with Henry Hurwitz, and helped precipitate what an old friend of Hurwitz's, a former contributor to the magazine, called "the end of the merry detour," when Cohen was laid off in 1931.[17]

Cohen also followed the lead of the former Associate Editor, Marvin Lowenthal, by encouraging the publication of European literature written by Jews about Jewish experience or topics of Jewish interest. Lowenthal took up residence in Paris in 1924, and ran a branch office of the *Menorah*

Journal from his apartment there. He brought the work of Andre Spire, Iwan Goll, Louis Zangwill, Louis Golding, Philip Guedalla, and others to the pages of the *Journal*, as well as the reproduction of many works of art by European Jewish artists. His solicitations for articles were bold: On an earlier trip he had approached Freud, and he introduced Hurwitz to the work of Martin Buber ("We think Buber is great stuff"), when Clifton Fadiman finally translated some "Sayings of the Baal-Shem-Tov" in 1929, after Lowenthal had become estranged from Hurwitz, it marked one of the earliest introductions of the American audience to the work of the German thinker. A European trip which Fadiman made in the summer of 1927 was responsible for securing the contributions of the German playwright and novelist Lion Feuchwanger, which Fadiman translated; and on a suggestion of Elliot Cohen's, Fadiman translated several legends of the Ari from Chaim Bloch's *Kabbalistische Sagen*, which had just been published at Leipzig in 1925.[18]

Then, most characteristically, Cohen encouraged humor, which for him was a principle of community; and satire, which his disappointed idealism made an imperative mode of expression.

In 1929, a committee of seven (including Elliot Cohen, Louis Berg, Fadiman, Solow, and Trilling) sent out a letter on stationery printed especially for the occasion (with Cohen's home address on the letterhead), announcing the formation of Lishmoh ("for its own sake")—"The Sampsin Gideon Memorial Association: For the Promotion and Perpetuation of Jewish Conviviality and the Celebration of the Pleasanter Jewish Festivals." Sampson Gideon, the eighteenth-century British financier and lover of the arts, probably appealed to Cohen's waggish and subversive sense of Jewish identity: Gideon resigned from his synagogue when the Jews' Naturalization Bill (1753) was repealed and continued public connection with the Jewish community would have been a social and professional liability; but it was discovered on his death that he had contiued his financial subscriptions to Jewish organizations under an assumed name. The gilded Marrano Gideon was resurrected by the group to be its patron spirit. The "Association" proposed to meet weekly—besides attending Hurwitz's official Menorah dinners, as invited—"to look upon each other's faces, to eat a sound meal, to drink beer, and to engage in an evening of Jewish, that is high (and loud) conversation on the state of America in the Reign of Hoover and the health of the universe."

Sometimes as many as fifty Jewish artists, writers, and intellectuals would gather in one evening, on Irving Place in rooms over a German beer garden; or in Meyer's Hotel in Hoboken, where they once staged a Yiddish puppet show; or in speakeasy Italian restaurants like Del Pezzo's in a private home on 71st Street, which was perhaps the location of the violent and amicable debate on Jewish nationalism Cohen recalled between Shmarya Levin and Sidney Hook. It was a "moveable feast"—a traveling Jewish Algonquin circle of wits.[19]

Cohen encouraged the community of comedy in the pages of the *Journal* as well, noting at the inauguration of his "Commentaries" section that he was "especially anxious for material of humorous or satirical intent, either in prose or verse." Cohen published the furious satire of Henry Rosenthal, another Columbia graduate; and Fadiman's sketches of Jewish families that, culturally adrift, fanatically adopt the coloration of musicality or high Russian culture as their identity. The 1920s was the era of Jewish vaudeville, of the Marx Brothers, Eddie Cantor, Sophie Tucker, Al Jolson, Georgie Jessel, and Fannie Brice. And Cohen's magazine in that explosive comedic spirit took on Jewish cultural shame and the absurdity of behavior following from it that he found endemic in the immigrant and his own generation.[20]

Between February 1924 and November 1927, a feature of each issue was Cohen's compilation of facts and quotations from the press concerning Jewish life which he ironically juxtaposed, and sent out with the anguish and hope of letters in a bottle, calling his collections "Notes for a Modern History of the Jews." Swapping clippings from the Jewish and general press—especially "Rabbinical exhibits" of rhetoric—as evidence of the comic absurdity of the Jewish cultural situation, had been a habit of Henry Hurwitz and Adolph Oko, the librarian of the Hebrew Union College, a contributing editor of the *Menorah Journal* during the war. Cohen embraced the clipping as a kind of found literature—an indigenous comic genre. "An Elder of Zion," a persona Cohen assumed in the *Journal* in 1929, was also addicted to cutting tidbits out of the Jewish press, and is described with his

> hands shaking, a strange gleam in his eyes, his body bent over a table on which there lies a copy of The American Hebrew, ... rummag(ing) fanatically among its columns. Look how he mumbles to himself, uttering now and again startled incredulous cries of discovery, looking up with the harried preoccupation of a collector whose nose scents the indubitable overpowering reek of buried treasure-trove.
>
> Pity him. It is a strange, morbid voice, and he is sore beset.[21]

What Cohen found in the record of American Jewish life in the 20s were the contradictions and confusions not yet sorted by sociology, nor resolved by the passage of time. Cohen took this variegated Jewish life into himself; his "Notes" record an activity of both criticism and engagement.

His typical strategy was to juxtapose the contradictory statements of different Jews of prominence, like this:

> Louis Marshall, testifying before the Senate Immigration Committee, informed the Committee that if the immigration quota law had been in effect when his father came to America he would have been barred from entering. *** Samuel Gompers sent a special communication to all organized labor unions urging support of the Johnson Immigration Restriction Bill as "of the greatest importance to the interests of humanity in general and labor in particular."
>
> "I have found Yiddish to be the most useful language which a man can know in

his travels. It deserves to be the language of diplomacy."—William Seagle. * * * "I am opposed to Yiddish, which I do not regard as a language but as a by-product of tea and pickles."—Rabbi Joel Blau.

"I believe that . . . the Jew can better contribute to the world's cultural advancement by intermarrying"—Louis Untermeyer. * * * "The newspapers carried headlines to the effect that Irving Berlin was married. But to whom was he married? To Miss Ellin MacKay, a member of the elite aristocracy of America, not a Jewess but a Catholic . . . Berlin must be blessed with a powerfully magnetic personality—his features are strikingly Jewish — to have been able to win such a wife . . . (But we yearn to return home. The rich man who visits his poor kinsfolk enjoys the rye bread and herring more than his own delicacies in his palatial home; Berlin's wife will at some future time long to count her beads. Shema Yisroel cannot mix with Ava Maria."—Rabbi Morris Teller.[22]

The spectacle was delicious, and no small part of the irony was generated by holding the grandiose claims made for Jewry from certain "modern" pulpits against the actual facts of Jewish life: Immediately after citing Rabbi Nathan Krass' statement that "The Jews exist to safeguard monotheism for the world," Cohen points out that Joseph and "Whitey" Diamond have just confessed to murdering two bank messengers in Brooklyn. When the *American Israelite* of Cincinnati claims that Judaism is "a system of ethics, pure and simple and its code is the basis of the highest existing form of civilization," Cohen quietly notes an item in the *Jewish Guardian* which says that "nearly all the leaders of the Fascisti party in Italy are Jews." Then Again, there were the claims of anti-Semites to hold against reality: Cohen juxtaposed the assertion about the Jew's physical inferiority with a clipping about the success of boxer Benny Leonard. And there were the contradictions of the facts of life themselves: More than forty new synagogues were built in 1925, yet another observer claimed that attendance at services was down.[23]

Cohen was excited by the small incidents that registered Orthodoxy's accommodation to modernity; they stimulated his sense of incongruity—like the first certificate of kashrut granted a mass-produced cracker in 1925, and the civil law-suit brought by an Orthodox congregation in Cleveland against its rabbi for instituting religious reforms. Most of all, he was sensitive to the gap between the glory claimed for Jewish life and its middle-class vulgarization. He was a heartsick chronicler of the programmed indignity of synogogues and Jewish Centers, and the folly of bourgeois values. His eye caught the advertisement for an electrically illuminated wedding canopy in the Jewish *Boston Advocate;* notice of a bathing-beauty contest held at the South Shore Temple in Chicago; the Toledo *Israelite's* delighted report of a Jewish party in Saskatoon in which all the adults came dressed as children. To David Belasco's observations that box-office receipts were down on the High Holidays, so Jewish "religious observances and their fealty" must still be strong, Cohen juxtaposed the Associated Press release on Rabbi Earnest R. Trattner of Temple Emanu-El, who resigned his pulpit to become a motion picture director. "Rabbi Trattner in discussing his new work said: 'The church or synagogue and the motion picture have much in common. They share the same high ideals and the screen may have even a greater influence than the church. Because of its universal langugae, it has become the dominant force in Modern Civilization and therefore legitimately attracts, because of its broader scope, the erstwhile religious leader."[24]

Part folklorist, part disappointed lover, part comedian, Cohen also clipped items having about them the ironic wonder of the commonplace: A Jew recently married a Siamese princess; Moe Berg, shortstop for the Brooklyn Dodgers, studied Latin at the University of Paris between seasons; Irving Levine of Troop 204 in the Bronx won the Boy Scouts of America Harmonica contest held at Bear Mountain, New York; an eight-year-old boy of Belo Zerkow, Russia, brought suit against his parents for compelling him to study Hebrew; the Ku Klux Klan of Alexandria, Louisiana, recently cooperated in welcoming to the City the Convention of District Grand Lodge No. 7 of the B'nai B'rith; Arthur J. Kuhn wrote a paper on Dante's Jewish origin, noting as evidence the poet's use of Old Testament characters and the fact that he never makes anti-Jewish remarks; Morris Fisher of the U.S. Marines—a Jew!—won the individual rifle championship of the world.[25]

What fuels this humor are the stereotypes of Jews—both of Jewish and gentile manufacture, against which, and *despite* which the individual lives of Jews continue to be lived out in unpredictable normalcy. Cohen impiously challenged the terms of particularly Jewish discourse claimed for the folk, whether impossibly grand or habitually self-deprecatory. When Jews could rise above shlemiehlhood to marry **Siamese princesses**, and forget their religious mission long enough to win harmonica contests—while their leaders talked in the nonsense of generalities—then only the actual lives of Jews became significant, and not any psuedo-traditional ideas about them. Cohen had a feel for the folk, and taught Lionel Trilling, for one, that an intellectual life was not incompatible with a passionate sense of democracy and a strong taste for the people's culture.[26]

The genius of Cohen's managing editorship of the *Menorah Journal* lay in his great gift as a teacher. He was a stimulator of thought, a professional mentor. While he was at Yale, the Department of English was noted for the enthusiastic force of its teaching. Though the graduate course in methodology required a knowledge of German, so that the students might fully master the principles of philology, and the classically-weighted curriculum required Old English, the vigorous faculty had long since inititated courses in more contemporary literature and practical composition. William Lyon Phelps had already been teaching his pioneering course on American Literature for more than twenty years when Cohen came to Yale, and he also taught contemporary drama. Canby offered a survey course in the short story which concluded with the students themselves writing fiction as well as criticism. Canby's course in Literary Compostion included "training in editorial service"; and Frederick E. Pierce offered a course in Contemporary Poetry.[27]

Phelps was the most flamboyant teacher on the English faculty, enthusiastically spreading the gospel of contemporaniety from the lecture platform as well as in the classroom. (He was the Lyceum lecturer who had radicalized Randolph Bourne with a lecture on the modern novel.) Though apparently wary of Phelp's showmanship (Cohen, who had had several courses with him, once referred to the prospect of his company at a musical evening, as hearing "Billy Phelps on the Billy Phelps"), Cohen responded to Phelp's enthusiasm as a method. Both Cohen and Phelps shared what Canby noted as characterizing the school of enthusiasm,"not so much oratory or histrionics as an uncritical faith in the miracle of knowledge." About teaching, Phelps wrote:

> Minute and exact accuracy must sometimes be sacrificed for emphasis. . . . A teacher who teaches with constant parentheses, qualifications, and trivial explanations will never make any definite impression. . . . If a teacher wishes to succeed with pupils, he must inflame their imaginations. The lesson should put the classroom under the spell of an illusion, like a great drama.[28]

The *Menorah Journal* under Cohen, as well as the early *Commentary*, were unlike most magazines in that a young writer not only displayed, but learned his craft through his association.[29]

Because of the intensity of Cohen's devotion to the work of his friends, there came a time when developing writers had to break away from his influence. Cohen's tragedy was that of other extraordinary teachers—he himself found it tortuous to write, as if conversation alone were sufficiently protean to communicate all he perceived. Cohen's nature reminded Louis Berg of what was said of Macaulay, that he was a perfectionist who, having proved his case, kept thinking up new arguments. Tess Slesinger, whose short stories and reviews were the most significant contribution of a woman to the *Menorah Journal* under Cohen's editorship, left the group—and her husband Herbert Solow—in the early 1930's. *The Unpossessed* (1934) is her novel criticizing her experience with the *Menorah* men. In it, the profoundest attribute of the character clearly meant to represent Cohen is his ability to make personal decisions:

> No Jew, he reflected, could see things so straight, so clear; no Jew, if he was besieged by thoughts, could set the thoughts aside and leap, unhindered. A Jew, if he had any brains at all, had twice as much as anyone else; he saw all sides at once and so his hands were tied, his brain stood still, he couldn't leap here and he couldn't leap there.[30]

Some writers who learned from Cohen —Tess Slesinger included—came to feel that in the rigor of his demand for revision, he was writing through them, performing an act of ventriloquism. The satire Cohen wrote for the *Menorah Journal* (that was not simply the artful arrangement of clippings) had to be torn from him; he was never quite finished rethinking and revising the pieces. Irwin Edman, whose series of sketches on Reuben Cohen (a "typical" Jewish college student) Elliot Cohen had urged him to write, acknowledged the liberating manipulation:

> I am very grateful for your most helpful suggestions. I am almost certain you should really be doing the thing instead of I. But if I plagiarize your ideas now and then, you have brought it on yourself.[31]

A draft of the first article Elliot Cohen wrote after joining the staff, a review of the second Menorah Summer School in 1923, illuminates his impasse: only on pages eight and nine of an eighteen-page typescript is there any actual description of the summer school curriculum and faculty; the rest is abstract observation about the place of the Jew in the modern world, the need for systematized Jewish knowledge available to the layman, the nature of "the Jewish mind." Cohen's gift was for ideas and the tropes of speculation. He was incapacitated as a writer to the extent that he spun abstract arguments between himself and a clear and unified perception of his subject. He was caught in the stimulus of evasion.[32]

Cohen was not scholarly, not always reliable on the points of fact he advanced with confidence; but he was intimate with the workings of mind, and was an incisive, intuitive critic. To the degree that his mind evaded the exposition of content, it was sensitive to the techniques and assumption of argument. In his digression on the Jewish mind in his summer school essay, he redefines the "true Menorah ideal" for himself as the "sheer fun involved in the sportive play of the intellect": "A meeting between minds should more nearly resemble a rodeo than an undertaker's parlor." He continued, having learned from Phelps:

> ... specific facts, no matter how thoroughly learned, become dim and the most enthusiastic scribblings in notebooks lose their primal fire. But these things will remain: the perception of keen, flashing flexible minds, distinctive in their individual frettings, but alike in their fine high temper, attacking, playing about, as a foil might in the hands of an expert fencer, the problems that confront and resist human thought, the inspiring realization that study can be detached without being cold, that learning can be scholarly and not dry, that the intellectual life offers not only a complete and wholehearted expression of the individual self, but an increasing source of pleasure and delight as well.[33]

Starting from such an early conviction about the nature of "the Jewish mind," Cohen encouraged a Jewish literature neither scholarly nor religious nor Zionist, but avowedly Jewish for the scintillating passion of its style. His overt intention was to bring into being a literature that would regard American Jewish life with a clear literary and journalistic eye, and that would temper the piety of survivalism with humor. This he did. One of the most improtant contributions of his editorship was sociological, for he understood his job to involve the invention of a certain kind of Jewish intellectual community. First inspired by the enterprise of Henry Hurwitz, Elliot Cohen made it possible for a writer to have a serious literary career, and stay Jewish by association, if not always by virtue of a dominating intellectual interest.

FOOTNOTES

The abbreviation HHMA refers to the Henry Hurwitz Menorah Association Memorial Collection, American Jewish Archives, Cincinnati, Ohio.

[1] On his name: Cohen in interview with Fern Marja, "Commentary's Number One Editor," New York *Post*, 17 February 1949, Mag. Sec., p. 1.

On his birthplace: Published sources often give Cohen's birthplace as Des Moines, where his birth is on record, but his family believes he was born in Tama, where his parents were then living, a doctor from the capital city being called in to assist the difficult delivery. See, for example, biographical note, *Menorah Journal (MJ)* 4 (October 1918), 278; Yale Yearbook, p. 105; Sylvia Cohen, interview; Cohen, Letter to Iowa Bureau of Vital Statistics, 15 May 1930, HHMA, box 7, folder 15.

Samuel Ettelson: "Biographical Data on Harry W. Ettelson," MS, by Harry Ettelson, in Biographies File — H. W. Ettelson, AJA; Cohen in Marja, p. 1. According to his son, Samuel Ettelson called his collection *Udim mutsalim* — that is, twigs pulled from the fire, or survivors; Elsa Ruth Herron, interview, 20 June, 1976.

[2] Elsa Ruth Herron, interview; Trilling, interview with Novack, February 1974. Both "H. Cohen" and "S. Ettelson" were paying members of Mobile's Reform Congregation in 1907 — *Congregation Shaarei Shomayim, Mobile, Alabama: Dedication of the New Temple* [program], 21-23 June 1907, in AJA.

[3] Cohen in Marja interview:
"My background isn't unusual. It's par for the course. It isn't me. It's all American Jews who come, by and large, from people with intellectual capacities or ambitions. In my case, they had both. They came to America to be good Americans and good Jews and keep store. Macy's and Gimbel's across the street began that way."

Cohen attended high school at Barton Academy, Mobile — Elsa Ruth Herron, interview.

[4] Cohen's father was born in 1870: Yale Yearbook, p. 105; Sylvia Cohen, interview; Trilling, interview with Novack, February 1974; Elsa Ruth Herron, interview. Cohen married Sylvia Kantrowitz of New Haven on 19 June 1929. Their son Tom Elliot Cohen was born 11 March 1935: *Fifty Year Album*, p. 65.

[5] Elsa Ruth Herron, interview; Cohen in Marja interview; telephone interview with Diana Trilling, 7 June 1976; Mandel Cohen, "Books for Little Bernard," *MJ*, 15 (July 1928), 191-2. There were five Cohen children: Elliot, Myra, Annette (Robinson), Mandel, and Elsa Ruth (Herron).

[6] Elsa Ruth Herron, interview.

[7] Cohen, Letter to Hurwitz, 11 June 1923, Henz Hurwitz Menorah Archives (HHMA), American Jewish Archives, Cincinnati, Ohio, box 7, folder 14. Cohen At Yale: telephone interview with Mabel DeVane, 19 June 1976; letter received from Judith A. Schiff (Chief Research Archivist, Yale University Library), 17 June 1976; Yale Yearbook, Class of 1918, pp. 105-106; Marja, p. 1.

On his projected dissertation: Sylvia Cohen, interview; Mabel DeVane, interview, June 1976. Cohen, Letter to Margaret T. Corwin (Executive Secretary to the Graduate School), 15 February 1923; "Graduate School-Scholarship Record"; Chauncy Tinker, Letter to W. L. Cross, 28 January 1921, all in Elliot Cohen files, Yale Graduate School, Office of the Registrar.

Cohen on Tinker: James and Elsa Grossman, interview; Cohen's feeling of exclusion: DeVane, interview.

Cohen wrote of his undergraduate career:
"I 'majored' while in College in Philosophy and Psychology. I was freed to do this because the majority of the courses which I proposed to take in English in Senior year were not given. Also, I did not have the time to finish the required minor in German. English however, is the subject in which I have always planned to specialize."
— Cohen, hand-written note, Yale Records. I am grateful to Elsa Ruth Herron for permitting me access to Cohen's university record.

[8]Cohen and Luce: Louis Berg, interview; Yale Yearbook, Class of 1918, pp. 105-106, and Phelps' essay; Cohen's prize essay: "The Promise of the American Synagogue," *MJ*, 9 (October 1918), 278-286, and (December 1918), 368-374.

Perhaps Cohen's reserve was not untypical of the behavior of immigrants' children at Yale in his generation; looking back from 1936 on life at Yale, Canby recalled romantically:
"Another and very different type of industrious student in those classes is well recognized now, but then was regarded by the pink and well soaped elect as just another undesirable. The second generation from the East of Europe was beginning to come to college: — Polish Jews with anemic faces on which were set dirty spectacles, soft-eyed Italians too alien to mix with an Anglo-Saxon community, seam-faced Chinese.... Occasionally [in class] there would be a revelation of intellect or a hint of the future when... some Rsssian Jewish exile asked to comment on an Ibsen play, and losing control of his guarded intellect, would expound a social philosophy that made the class squirm as if a blast of fire had scorched the seats of their comfortable pants."
— Canby, *Alma Mater: The Gothic Age of the American College* (New York: Farrar & Rinehart, 1936), pp. 128-129.

[9]The move to 63 Fifth Avenue was made between mid-1926 and mid-1927: see the letterheads, HHMA, box 7, folders 14 and 15, passim.

Telephone interview with Frances (Grossel) Reiss, 24 May 1976; Albert Halper, *Good-bye, Union Square: A Writer's Memoir of the Thirties*, (Chicago: Quadrangle, 1970), p. 28; personal interview with Irving and Mae (Wechsler) Jurow, 8 June 1976; Trilling, "Young in the Thirties," *Commentary*, 41 (May 1966), 45.

[10]Telephone interview with F. Reiss; Mae Jurow, interview; Trilling, *A Gathering of Fugitives* (Boston: Beacon, 1956), p. 49.

Hurwitz: Personal interview with David Hurwitz, 6 June 1976.

The Village: Susan Edmiston and Linda D. Cirino, *Literary New York: A History and Guide* (Boston: Houghton, 1976), pp. 105-110; personal interview with Harry Starr, 4 June 1976.

[11]Mae Jurow, interview; Trilling, "Young in the Thirties," 45.

There is no single collection of Cohen's papers from which to write his story, according to his widow, Sylvia Cohen, and Francis Green, who confirmed the destruction of his *Commentary* correspondence. Personal interview with Sylvia Cohen, 14 February 1976; telephone interview with Francis Green, 1 June 1976.

Podhoretz, *Making It* (New York: Random, 1967), p. 134; Cohen, Memo to Hurwitz, n.d. (c. March 1926), HHMA, box 9, folder 14.

[12]Edman, Letters to Hurwitz, 31 May 1928, and 8 August 1928, both in HHMA, box 9, folder 15; personal interview with Louis Berg, 25 September 1975.

[13]Trilling, "Young in the Thirties," 45; personal interview with Felix Morrow, 9 February 1976; Mayrowitz, "Golden Jubilee: The Story of Brownsville," *MJ*, 14 (June 1928), 583 ff.; Halper, *Good-bye, Union Square*, pp. 28-31; Irving Jurow, interview; telephone interview with Mable DeVane, 20 September 1976.

[14]Trilling introduced Fadiman to the *Menorah Journal* staff by letter: Trilling, Letter to Cohen, 3 April 1926, HHMA, box 59, folder 10.

Anecdote: Personal interview with Albert Halper, 11 February 1976.

Elliot Cohen as editor: Personal interview with Elsa Ruth (Cohen) Herron and Davis Herron, 20 June 1976; Trilling, "Young in the Thirties," 45; Irving Jurow, interview.

Trilling first regarded Cohen's passion for simplicity as Philistine, but gradually learned its wisdom. — William Novack, unpublished interview with Lionel Trilling, 12 February 1974. I am very grateful to Mr. Novack for making this and other interviews concerning Elliot Cohen available to me.

Personal interview with Salo Baron, 29 June 1976; Solow continued to advise Baron concerning the style of the early volumes of his *Social and Religious History of the Jews*.

Meyer Levin, *In Search: An Autobiography* (New York: Pocket-Simon & Schuster, 1973), pp. 23-24; Halper, *Good-bye, Union Square*, pp. 275, 122, 57; personal interview with Marie Syrkin,

17 February 1976.

[15] For the inauguration of "Commentaries" see *MJ*, 10 (August-September 1924), 401; Podhoretz, p. 133; Clement Greenberg and Robert Warshow also objected to the fiction Cohen published in *Commentary* — Irving Kristol, interview with William Novack, 13 May 1974; Louis Berg, interview; Berg, "Out of the Mouths of Babes," *MJ*, 14 (March 1928), 306 ff.; "The Voice of the Bridegroom," *MJ*, 18 (February 1930), 163 ff.; "Old Man Reshinsky," *MJ*, 17 (December 1929), 276 ff; David Bergelson, "The Revolution and the Zussmans," trans. Berg, *MJ*, 17 (December 1929), 239 ff.

[16] For the inauguration of "Chronicles" see *MJ*, 14 (January 1928), 85; Berg, "The J.D.C. Holds a Conference," *MJ*, 16 (June 1929), 546 ff.; Herbert Solow, "The Vindication of Jewish Idealism," *MJ*, 15 (September 1928), 259 ff.; Berg, "American Public Opinion on Palestine," *MJ*, 17 (October 1929), 67 ff.; Berg, "The Palestine Press and the Attacks," *MJ*, 17 (November 1929), 170 ff.; Philip S. Bernstein, "Roumania Backslides" *MJ*, 19 (November-December 1930), 172 ff.; Irving Fineman, "The Incident at Petach Tikvah: Class Struggle in Palestine," *MJ*, 16 (January 1929), 64 ff.; Benjamin Glassberg, "The Philanthropy Boom Collapses," *MJ*, 19 (June 1931), 434 ff.; Abraham Revutsky, "Bira-Bidzhan: A Jewish Eldorado?" *MJ*, 16 (February 1929), 158 ff.; Sarah C. Schack, "The Kosher Chicken Racket," *MJ*, 18 (February 1930), 148 ff.; William Schack, "The Conquest of Sea Gate," *MJ*, 18 (January 1930), 52 ff.

[17] HHMA, box 56, folder 7, passim; Nathan Isaacs, Letter to Cohen, 17 October 1931, HHMA, box 21, folder 4.

[18] Marvin Lowenthal, Letter to Hurwitz, 21 November 1925, HHMA, box 32, folder 9; Lowenthal, Letter to Hurwitz, 23 December 1922, HHMA, box 32, folder 8.

Fadiman, Letter to S. S. [?] and Cohen, 23 September 1927; Fadiman, Letter to Cohen, 16 January 1928; Cohen, Letter to Fadiman, 2 September 1926; Fadiman, Letter to Cohen, n.d. [begins: "I have read one of the books . . ."], all in HHMA, box 11, folder 2.

Fadiman, trans., "Sayings of the Baal-Shem Tov," *MJ*, 17 (October 1929), 52 ff.; "Conversations With the Wandering Jew," by Feuchtwanger, *MJ*, 14 (February 1928), 128 ff; "Legends of the Ari," by Chaim Bloch, *MJ*, 14 (April 1928), 371 ff., and (May 1928), 466 ff.

[19] Louis Berg, Letter to Hurwitz, 12 December 1929, HHMA, box 7, folder 15; "Gideon, Sampson," *Universal Jewish Encyclopedia*; Cohen, "The Intellectuals and the Jewish Community," 21; Hurwitz, Letter to Fadiman, 5 October 1926, HHMA, box 11, folder 2; personal interview with James and Elsa Grossman.

[20] *MJ*, 10 (August-September 1924), 401; Fadiman, "A la Russe," *MJ*, 12 (June-July 1926), 313 ff.; "The Musical Krotkys," *MJ*, 12 (August-September 1926), 418 ff.

[21] Oko, Letter to Hurwitz, 10 November 1919, HHMA, box 38, folder 14; see also Oko, Letter to Hurwitz 13 December 1918, HHMA, box 38, folder 12; Hurwitz, Letter to Oko, 19 March 1920, HHMA, box 39, folder 1.

Cohen, "Marginal Annotations," *MJ*, 18 (February 1930), 171.

[22] Cohen, "Notes for a Modern History of the Jews," *MJ*, 11 (June-July 1924), 298; (February 1925), 75; 12 (April-May 1926), 194.

[23] "Notes," *MJ*, 10 (February 1924), 82; 12 (April-May 1926), 193, 192; (June-July 1926), 308.

[24] "Notes," *MJ*, 11 (April 1925), 179; (June 1925), 283 — the rabbi was Solomon Goldman of the Cleveland Jewish Center; 12 (April-May 1926), 193, 192; 11 (June-July 1924), 297; 13 (February 1927), 77.

[25] "Notes," *MJ*, 10 (February 1924), 82; (April-May 1924), 185; (November-December 1924), 509; 11 (April 1925), 179; 13 (November 1927), 510; 11 (February 1925), 74.

[26] Trilling, "Young in the Thirties," 45.

[27] *Catalogue of the Graduate School*, Yale University, 1918/1919, pp. 76-83, 1921/1922, p. 93; Laurence Vesey, *The Emergence of the American University* (Chicago: University of Chicago Press, 1965), p. 224; Pierson, Vol. I, pp. 269 ff., 355 ff. Pierce found Cohen's work in Contemporary Poetry "irregular," and failed him: "Graduate School — Scholarship Record," and F. E. Pierce, note to Margaret Corwin, written on Cohen to Corwin, 23 July 1920, Yale records.

[28] Bourne, "History of a Literary Radical," *Yale Review*, 8 (April 1919), 468-484; "Graduate School — Scholarship Record"; DeVane, interview, September 1976; Canby, p. 121; Phelps, *Teaching in School and College*, pp. 96-7, 51.

[29] Personal interview with Daniel Bell, 19 January 1976.

[30] Cohen as editor and writer manqué: Trilling, "Young in the Thirties," 45; personal interview with Diana Trilling, 10 February 1976; Louis Berg, interview with Diana Trilling, 10 February 1976; Louis Berg, interview; Tess Slesinger, *The Unpossessed* (New York: Simon & Schuster, 1934), p. 33.

[31] Personal interview with Daniel Bell, 19 January 1976; Louis Berg, interview; Edman, Letter to Cohen, 31 March 1926, HHMA, box 9, folder 14.

[32] "The Menorah Summer School: A New Agency for Liberal [sic] Education," HHMA, box 7, folder 17; published form: "The Menorah Summer School: A New Agency for Liberal Education," *MJ*, 9 (October 1923), 338-343.

[33] Trilling, interview with William Novack, February 1974; Diana Trilling, interview; Cohen, Menorah Summer School draft, pp. 13-15.

Saul Bellow is supposed to have said that reading Cohen's prose was like washing your feet with your socks on: Irving Howe, unpublished interview with William Novack, 15 May 1974.

From Russia to America: Baruch Charney Vladeck and the Evolution of Jewish Socialism

Franklin Jonas

Baruch Charney Vladeck
(1886-1938)
Courtesy of the Bund Archives,
New York

This article deals with the transition from Russia to America of the Jewish socialist, Baruch Charney Vladeck. A prominent figure in the Jewish Labor Bund during the Revolution of 1905, Vladeck emigrated to America in 1908 where he immediately became active in the Jewish labor and socialist movements. Adapting readily to American conditions, he emerged as a major figure in the Jewish community during and after World War I. From 1918 to 1938, he was manager of the *Jewish Daily Forward,* the influential and labor-oriented Yiddish daily in New York City; and with this position as his base, he became involved in virtually every area of concern to Jewish labor.

At the time of his death in 1938, Vladeck was serving at one and the same time as Chairman of the Jewish Labor Committee, President of People's ORT, executive board member of HIAS and of the Joint Distribution Committee, leader of the La Guardia coalition in New York's City Council, and as an activist in the public housing movement.[1]

According to Daniel Bell, Vladeck's career "symbolizes the transformations wrought by American institutions on a European-shaped radicalism."[2] If Vladeck's life-work is as representative as Bell thinks, then it follows that a study of his early career promises to provide insight into the evolution of Jewish socialism in the United States. It is the writer's contention that the changes in Vladeck's ideology and politics after he emigrated to the United States were not drastic and that there was great coherence and continuity in the development of his socialism.

Baruch Nachman Charney[3] was born on January 13, 1886 in Dukor, Lithuania, about 30 miles from the growing industrial city of Minsk. Dukor was a typically impoverished and deeply religious community of the Russian Pale,[4] consisting of about 100 Jewish families who obtained their livelihoods from artisanry and petty commerce.[5] Baruch's father, Wolf, was a grain and leather merchant who died when the boy was three, leaving his widow to raise alone their brood of five boys and one girl, among whom Baruch was the fifth eldest and the fourth son.[6]

In spite of the family's deepening poverty, the five Charney brothers, like most Jewish boys in Eastern Europe, were schooled rigorously in religion. The Jews of Dukor adhered to the Hasidism of Lubavitch, a sect that combined Kabalist mysticism with traditional Orthodoxy. "I went three times a day to synagogue," Charney would later recall "and the rest of the time to school."[7]

When Baruch was ten, poverty forced his mother to break up her family. He and his brother Samuel, who was two years older, were sent to Minsk where they enrolled in a yeshiva to begin preparing for the rabbinate. In this thriving industrial city of 90,000, the two boys suffered a humiliating poverty which compelled them to pay for their cramped two-to-a-bed lodging by tutoring other students and to obtain their meals by "eating days," a system of charity in which well-off Jewish families took turns in providing meals once a week to one or two rabbinical students.[8]

In Minsk, Baruch and Samuel came gradually under the influence of secular Russian literature and of political ideology. Many of their classmates were secretly reading Russian books which were strictly forbidden by the rabbis; and soon the Charney brothers were following their example. As a teenager, Baruch attended classes in science taught by Gregory Garshuni, a chemist and a leader of the Social Revolutionary Party who had organized the campaign of assassination which took a heavy toll among Czarist officials around the turn of the century. It was Gershuni who persuaded the boy that "there is no future in studying the dead books of a dead past." At the age of 15, Baruch Charney abandoned his religious studies and moved into another residence far from the yeshiva.[9]

He now began to study on his own, earning his livelihood by tutoring and by working in a semi-private library. Like thousands of other young Jewish externs (people who studied without attending a school), Baruch Charney felt resentment and alienation toward a regime that was denying him an education while in myriad ways discriminating against and systematically oppressing the Jews.[10] Unable to envisage a tolerable future under the Czarist regime,[11] the externs of Minsk, Vilna, Warsaw, and other centers were readily recruited by the illegal radical and Zionist movements of the Pale.[12]

After quitting the yeshiva, Samuel and Baruch were often present at political discussions in the coffeehouses of Minsk and were gradually becoming involved with radical Zionism. At the age of 16, Baruch joined the Poale Zion, a movement that advocated a homeland for the Jews in Palestine to be organized along socialist lines but also favored a revolution within the Russian Empire. "In those days," he would later recall, "I was most at home with circles which tried to combine the flaming torch of revolution with the little man on the donkey."[13]

In January, 1904, Baruch, who for some weeks had been teaching political economy to a group of trade school students, was arrested on the charge of spreading subversive ideas among the young. He spent the next eight months in Minsk Prison[14] where he participated prominently in several acts of resistance to the prison authorities, including a hunger strike and a "mutiny" in which every breakable object in the cells of the political prisoners was smashed. There were dozens of "politicals" in the prison of a wide variety of political persuasions. The cells were left open during the day and there was incessant debate.

What he had heard and experienced in Minsk Prison converted Charney from Zionism to the teaching of the Jewish Labor Bund (the Jewish General Workers' Union of Russia, Poland, and Lithuania), a movement that agitated in Yiddish among the workers of the Pale and advocated both revolutionary socialism and the uncoerced development of Yiddish culture. "My best yeshiva," he later wrote, "was Minsk Prison where I saw clearly that the whole world order must be changed, that one must abolish class society which consists of oppressors and oppressed."[15]

For the next four years, Charney was an activist for the Bund. "I joined the movement," Charney later said, "as casually as a boy on the upper West Side joins the Democratic Party. You felt a tide was rising."[16] He took an active part in the organizing drives which succeeded for a time in building a true mass movement among the Jewish workers of the Pale. He addressed meetings, campaigned for Bundist candidates in the 1907 Duma elections, wrote for the party press, and was even involved, if only peripherally, with guerilla warfare and the distribution of weapons.[17] In addition to his earlier imprisonment in Minsk, Baruch Charney was captured and imprisoned on two other occasions: the first time at Lukishki Prison in Vilna from May to October, 1905 and the second in Lodz jail during the first six weeks of 1906.[18]

Charney functioned principally as an itinerant activist, moving quickly from city to city and assuming a different alias in each new place. He became well-known in the movement and among the Jewish workers as an orator and was nicknamed "the Second Lassalle" after the famous German orator and socialist leader of the 1860's. He addressed many public rallies and also spoke on weekends at the large mass-meetings that gathered secretly in the woods outside the Jewish towns that sometimes were attended by as many as 1000 people. Meyer Weisgal recalls in his autobiography having witnessed as a child several Bund rallies in the forest outside his hometown of Kikl in Poland and notes that the one addressed by "the Young Lassalle" was the largest ever.[19]

Charney rose quickly to prominence within the Bund. In July, 1906, he was placed in charge of the entire movement in Poland except for Warsaw and Lodz.[20] In May, 1907, he was a member of the Bund delegation at the meeting in London of the Russian Social Democratic Party where he dissented from the position taken by most of the other Bundist delegates, voting for a Bolshevik resolution on the aims of the movement and supporting Lenin's candidacy for the Central Committee. In later years, Charney would explain that in his uncertainty as to which form of organization was best, he had supported the man who seemed most sure of himself. "Lenin, the narrow-eyed Tartar ... appealed to my youthful romanticism. He seemed the man to blow life into the flickering embers of the revolution."[21]

Despite his apostasy at the conference, Charney became a close friend of Vladimir Medem, the chief spokesman and ideological leader of the Bund, writing for and helping him to edit *Di Naye Tsayt* the Bund's theoretical journal. He was also developing into a man of letters, publishing poetry and literary criticism which gained him the attention and friendship of important Yiddish writers such as Y. L. Peretz and Sholom Asch.[22] Charney's writings, some of them on religious subjects, suggest that in turning rebel against the Russian government, he, like many Bundists, had retained not only the Yiddish language but also many ties to his past.[23]

To Charney, as to the Bund generally, Yiddish culture was to be encouraged not primarily for its own sake but as an inextricable part of the liberation movement. Since the function of culture was to uplift the masses, "true cultural growth can take place only in the soil of the common life." These lines were written in refutation of an essay by Samuel Charney, Baruch's brother, in which, writing under the pen name S. Niger, he had disparaged popular culture and called for a purer approach to the arts.[24]

By 1908, the Czarist reaction had been mounting steadily in intensity for more than two years and most of Russia's revolutionary movements had fallen into disarray and impotence. Pursued relentlessly by the authorities, activists like Baruch Charney found it ever more difficult to avoid arrest. Reflecting that not even his name was his own and that there was scarcely a city in Russia or Poland where he was not hunted by the police, Charney decided, like many other Bundists in this period, to emigrate to the United States.[25] Two of his brothers had preceded him there and after they cabled him the money for his journey, he escaped to Belin and then went to Rotterdam. In mid-November, he sailed on the New Amsterdam, arriving in New York City on Thanksgiving Day, 1908.[26]

By the time of Baruch Charney's arrival in America, many of the nation's larger cities housed major Jewish enclaves where there were distinctive institutions and a somewhat separate way of life. Within these neighborhoods there were Yiddish speaking labor and socialist institutions that were beginning to take on added vitality due to the massive influx of newcomers from Eastern Europe. There were labor organizations, such as the United Hebrew Trades and various Yiddish speaking trade unions and also Yiddish speaking branches of the Socialist and Socialist Labor Parties, but the most successful of the Jewish radical insitutions as of 1908 were the Workmen's Circle, a fraternal order with a membership of 19,000 and the *Jewish Daily Forward,* a labor-oriented daily newspaper in New York City which claimed a circulation in excess of 75,000.

These overlapping but independent institutions formed an environment in which Vladeck[28] would thrive. Scarcely had he arrived in America than be began to deliver lectures in Yiddish before Jewish labor and socilalist organizations and to write for the Yiddish radical press. During his first four years in America, Vladeck earned his livelihood primarily as an itinerant lecturer. Traversing most of the United States and Canada, he addressed Workmen's Circle chapters, branches of the Socialist Party, and other organizations that were Yiddish-speaking and "progressive." The demand for Vladeck as a speaker rested in part on his reputation for effective oratory, but also on his first-hand knowledge of conditions in Russia. His lectures dealt chiefly at first with events in Russia, but he spoke as well on abstract literary subjects and dealt increasingly with aspects of the American scene.[29] Often, there were people in the audience who had first heard him in Russia or Poland at the secret meetings "in the woods" that had been arranged by the Bund.[30]

Vladeck had also begun to write for the Jewish socialist press in New York and Chicago. In 1909, he published polemical essays, poetry, and literary and theatrical criticism in *Der Arbeiter,* the Yiddish weekly of the Socialist Labor Party, the *Idishe Arbeiter Welt,* a Chicago weekly affiliated with Socialist Party, and in *Di Zukunft,* the monthly journal published in New York by the Forward Association. In 1910, he began to write for the

Jewish Daily Forward, the main pillar of the Jewish labor movement, the start of an association with that newspaper that ended only with his death in 1938.[31]

Like virtually all of the Bundist intellectual émigrés, Vladeck was critical of the existing Jewish labor and socialist movements which by early 1909 had succeeded in organizing only a small minority of the hundreds of thousands of Jewish workers in the United States. The movement's veteran leadership struck him as smug and complacent and to be doing all in their power to discourage the newly arrived socialists from participating in their movement. " 'We are experienced,' they say, 'we have been eating sandwiches and carrying on socialist work in America for twenty years'." His criticism of the movement was more pragmatic than it was theoretical, however, directed more at the paucity of its gains than at its methods or philosophy. "I know that I am still green," Vladeck wrote "and that to join any movement, one has to think much and study."[32]

His eagerness to participate in the labor and socialist movements of the United States made Vladeck unusual among Bundist intellectuals, for most of whom, after the danger, excitement, and passion of the revolutionary movement in Russia, life in the United States seemed crass and dull and the labor and socialist movements, both the Jewish and the American, hopelessly conservative.[33] Vladeck would later liken these disheartened émigrés, with their nostalgic longings for Russia and rejection of nearly all things American, to "chickens let loose on a foreign chicken yard."[34]

In September, 1909, Vladeck joined the Socialist Party and in December, he was appointed by the Jewish Agitation Bureau, an association of the party's Yiddish speaking branches, to the post of Organizer.[35] For the next two and one-half years, he was a travelling activist for the bureau who lectured, sold literature, and strove in general to get new Yiddish-speaking branches started. Although some of the more doctrinaire socialists, such as the Yiddish poet and radical, Morris Winchefsky, had dismissed the J. A. B. as too decentralized and lacking in autonomy to be effective, Vladeck, in his eagerness to take part in the movement in America hailed the bureau and predicted a great future for it.[36] In later years, however, he wrote of his organizing activity in this period as if it had all been a waste of time. "It makes me ill to look back. What I remember is foolish ... the first travelling agitator for the J. A. B. – the *hockemrashi* (chief wise man) who completely ruined the treasury."[37]

In November, 1909, Jewish trade unionism achieved its first major breakthrough in the great strike of the shirtwaist makers of New York City that is known as "the uprising of the twenty-thousand." In this dispute, which lasted more than three months, the strikers, mainly young Jewish and Italian women, won shorter working hours and better conditions, but only in the smaller shops; and they failed to win recognition for their union. Like many other veteran activists of the Jewish socialist movement, Vladeck took part in this strike as an organizer and also figured in certain of the later unionization drives among the Jewish workers in the garment trades.[35] In early March of 1910, Vladeck observed at first hand the general strike in Philadelphia where he found that multitudes of Jewish working men, including many who were Orthodox in religion, were joining the strike.[39]

To Vladeck, history seemed to be repeating itself. Having seen in Russia how the strikes and demonstrations of the 1890's had paved the way for the socialist-led mass movement of the 1900's, he predicted that in America, too, the largely spontaneous solidarity of the Jewish workers would sweep everything before it. "The Jewish worker will see for himself the need to create people, books, and means."[40]

During the autumn months of 1910, Vladeck managed the Workmen's Circle phase of Socialist Meyer London's bid to represent the Ninth District on New York's Lower East Side in the House of Representatives. London's managers were accused by disgruntled militants of showing Jewish voters how to vote for London while ignoring the rest of the Socialist ticket.[41] Although he indignantly denied this charge, Vladeck urged the Jewish socialists to learn from their hated enemy, the regular politicians, by keeping track of their supporters, so that they would not have to start from scratch in each new campaign. "Let us become politicians," he wrote, "I have no fear of the word."[42] He complained that the Bundist intellectuals were still keeping aloof from the political phase of the movement and appealed to them to participate in future campaigns. "Bring with you your sharp criticism, your religious wish, your youthful courage. Address me as a soldier would his comrade in the camp."[43]

During Vladeck's first two years in America, the Workmen's Circle doubled its national membership. Although impressed by the rapid growth of this fraternal order for the Jewish workers, Vladeck was highly critical of its educational programs which he regarded as "unplanned and chaotic." "On a list of lectures conducted in the course of the winter," he wrote in 1910, "you will find Jewish literature and free love, socialism and electricity, religion and canine teeth. One progressive branch even invited a Philadelphia rabbi to read from the Talmud." The major cause of the problem, Vladeck argued, was, paradoxically, the success of the order's insurance program which resulted in many becoming members who were neither radical nor politically idealistic.[44]

In *World of Our Fathers*, Irving Howe has claimed that Vladeck wrote of the Workmen's Circle "as though it were a radical party that has a right to demand discipline and coherence of belief."[45] While it is true that Vladeck considered these qualities as essential to the building of socialism, he never considered them to be attainable on demand. In the very essay that is cited by Howe, Vladeck states that what the Workmen's

Circle lectures should do is "assist the Jewish workers to work out their own attitudes toward life and mankind."[46] As he envisaged the movement, it would develop gradually into a "collective personality," progressive and yet spontaneous, disciplined and yet made of independent and enlightened individuals.[47] Had Vladeck considered it wise to require ideological conformity, he, like certain other Jewish socialists, would have urged the exclusion of businessmen from the Working Circle; but, in fact, he defended not only the inclusion of such members but even their occupying positions of leadership.[48]

Within two years of his arrival in America, however, Vladeck had become very doubtful of the prospects for Jewish socialism. While the Jewish trade unions had made major advances, politically, the movement seemed scarcely to have progressed at all. "It may be," wrote Vladeck in 1911, "and it seems to me that's how it will be, that a strong specifically Jewish socialist movement will never exist in America."[49] One indication was the strong support for the political machines among the Jewish working class voters. Moreover, among those Jewish immigrants who had risen into the middle class, many "had turned their backs on their former brothers and were fencing themselves off from their sufferings and problems."[50]

Vladeck's change of mind on the political prospects of the movement rested on an altered assessment of the Jewish working class immigrants. In their scramble for earnings, too many, he now believed, were remaining provincial and ignorant, failing even to learn English.[51] He also contended that their struggles in the United States had eroded the traditional sympathy for others that had been developed by the Jews over the centuries.[52] Of those reportedly mobile immigrants who were accommodating themselves to the American scene (the "all-rightniks," as they were called by the other Jews), many were assimilating in a hasty and superficial manner, "displaying a newly acquired mannerism which shocked with its false bravado and moronic self-confidence."[53]

The remedy did not lie in a revival of Jewish culture. On the question of "Yiddishkayt," Vladeck always adhered to the principle of "neutralism," a formula worked out by the Bund during the early 1900's, but repudiated by it after 1910. According to this doctirne, whether Jewish culture survived in the long run was a matter of indifference, so long as the cultural evolution of the Jews took place naturally and without coercion.[54] "If life every place, and in America in particular," he wrote in 1911, "should come to this: that the Jews should stop existing as a nation and in about 100 years, there would not be in America any Jewish schools, any Jewish newspapers, nor any Jewish writers, it would not bother me."[55]

Whatever the long-term prospects for Jewish culture in the United States, Vladeck was certain that the most useful immediate work for the Jewish socialists was to "de-green" the immigrants by assisting them to adapt constructively to American life. "The question before us is how to enrich his spiritual life, acquaint him with American life, and make him useful to himself and to America."[56] Vladeck looked primarily to the Workmen's Circle to provide the necessary instruction and uplift. "Through it," he wrote of the fraternal order in 1912, "the immigrant gains his first grasp of his duties as a citizen—cleanliness of body, tongue, and house and is slowly drawn into the wider world where he plays a role without being aware of it himself."[57] In emphasizing cleanliness and citizenship as his short-term goals for the immigrants, Vladeck was in essential agreement with the middle class and largely native born leadership of the settlement house and Americanization movements.

To be effective in America, Vladeck was convinced, "A socialist must be woven into the web of life here because the movement is before everything else, an American one."[58] Of all the Bundist intellectuals to settle in America, it was probably Vladeck who made the closest study of American conditions and the smoothest adjustment to life in the United States. From his earliest days in the United States, he had been preparing himself for an American career. As early as 1909, he was already conducting part of his correspondence in English and was also reading about certain aspects of American civilization. After becoming "travelling correspondent" of the *Forward,* Vladeck wrote on many aspects of the American scene, including Jewish life, the labor movement, and a series of reports on thirty-one American cities.[59] In June, 1911, he delivered his first public address in English at a Socialist Party picnic in Pittsburgh and discovered that despite his thick and guttural accent, he could be understood by an audience that knew only English.[60]

On August 14, 1911, Vladeck married Clara Richman of New York City. The daughter of a moderately prosperous Jewish merchant who had emigrated from Russia during the early 1900's, Clara was a trained nurse who had been one of the "girls in blue" in the famed visiting nurse service for the poor run by Lillian Wald at the Henry Street settlement. During the first seventeen months of their marriage, Vladeck remained a touring lecturer and journalist. In May, 1912, the couple had their first child, a daughter they named May, and that December, Vladeck moved his family to Philadelphia where he became the new business manager of the local branch of the *Jewish Daily Forward.*[61]

As manager of the *Forverts* in Philadelphia, Vladeck remained active in Yiddish-speaking labor and socialist movements. In June of 1912, the Jewish Agitation Bureau had been re-organized as the Jewish Socialist Federation which, like its predecessor, was affiliated with the Socialist Party but was to be far more centralized and effectively self-governing than the Bureau had been.[62] Although there was often hostility between the *Forward* establishment and J.S.F., which was led predominantly by radical emigres, Vladeck was somehow able to remain active within both organizations. In 1913, he was elected to the executive committee of the J.S.F. and in 1915, he was re-elected by a referendum of its members, receiving the second highest total of votes.[63]

Vladeck and his family remained in Philadelphia for more than three years, a span in which his roots in America steadily deepened. In 1914, Mrs. Vladeck gave birth to their second child, a son named William.[64] On April 7, 1915, Vladeck was granted citizenship in the Federal Court of the Eastern District of Pennsylvania.[65]

Eager to improve his abilities as a speaker and writer of English, Vladeck took courses for more than two years, commencing with the Fall semester of 1913, at the School of Education of the University of Pennsylvania. About half of his coursework was in English and Speech.[66] At the same time, he was continuing to read widely on American history and culture. By 1916, he was sufficiently versed in the nation's past to prepare a course on the subject for the "worker's university" program of the Workmen's Circle, and to write essays on the history of Tammany Hall and on the origins of American literature.[67]

In the summer of 1915, Vladeck was a candidate in the Philadelphia non-partisan primary for the office of judge of the Orphan's Court, receiving 6748 votes and coming in fourth.[68] Always an advocate of practicality in politics, he was by now thoroughly grounded in the standard methods of electioneering as it was practiced in America. The Socialists should not, he contended, base their campaigns on abstract idealism but on such "living questions as taxes, schools, parks, and labor laws." Aware of the value of personal ties in carrying elections, Vladeck appealed to the Jewish workers for loyalty (by voting Socialist) to "their own (nominally socialist) organizations." Like the professionals of the regular party organizations, he also recognized that the routine drudgery of canvassing and transporting one's supporters to the polls was of greater value in winning elections than the mass meetings and fiery speeches so fancied by radical activists.[69]

At times, Vladeck appealed for votes by blending his social idealism with ethnic consciousness. On one occasion, he assured his readers in the *Forverts* that Algernon Lee, a gentile who was a leading New York City Socialist and was then running for Congress, deserved their votes because "in his calm and courteous way," he fights "for a better America." According to Vladeck, "you could almost forget that he (Lee) is not a Jew." He even described Lee as "one of the 36 just men" who, according to Jewish legend, preserve the world through their piety and goodness.[70]

Like most American socialists of this period, Vladeck remained optimistic about the prospects of the movement in America. "I believe that I will see with my own eyes a socialist state in the United States," he wrote in 1916.[71] Conceding that the average American worker remained politically conservative, Vladeck drew comfort from the fact that some of the longest and bitterest strikes in history had taken place in the United States.[72]

In any case the same "laws of history" that functioned elsewhere were also at work in the United States. Although he wrote of "the social revolution" as inevitable, according to the "scientific" teachings of Karl Marx, Vladeck acknowledged that the belief of socialists like himself in a collectivist and democratic future was an act of faith, analogous in some respects to the belief of a pious Jew in the eventual coming of the promised messiah. Socialism thus became a sort of secularized Judaism in which one did numerous "good deeds" and patiently awaited the realization of the dream.[73]

By 1916, Vladeck felt that America was truly his home. He wrote appreciatively of the tradition of American idealism, "stretching from Roger Williams to Mother Jones, and admitted to having "prayed silently and without a hat in front of Independence Hall."[74] It is certainly significant that, unlike many other radicals from Russia, he never repatriated, not even after the two revolutions of 1917.[75]

"In front of me, lighting my way, sometimes with sunlight and sometimes with lightning, leading me forward, sometimes through perfumed pathways and sometimes through dirty, difficult paths, I see only one thing, America." Some of his feeling for the United States was awakened by his intoxication, as a romantic and a poet, with the beauty of the country's "natural wonders." As a Jew in Russia Vladeck had been confined by law and circumstances to the cities and towns of the Pale. "Here (in the United States), for the first time I felt free to explore the world as I want to see it ... I don't love it only as an artist for its colors, but as a citizen feeling that it is mine."[76] The awe and wonder with which he viewed nature reflected also the continuing influence on Vladeck of his upbringing when he had been taught to think of the natural world as God's handiwork and as the embodiment of His will.[77]

In spite of a growing tendency to regard himself as American, Vladeck's sense of being Jewish and his identification with the Jewish past were also growing stronger. "At no time have I felt more Jewish than I do now ... That special, ideal feeling of pride and pain which moved my forefathers now moves me too and no day passes that I don't think about how I should fit my Jewishness into the rest of me without being shattered in the process."[78] These feelings were strengthened by news of the sufferings of the Jews in Eastern Europe during World War I when hundreds of thousands were left homeless and were reduced to privation and hunger. "We hear," he wrote in 1915, "the quiet disheartened sighs of the men, the barely audible sobbing of the women. In our hearts is revived the old song: 'What we are, we are, but we are Jews' "[79]

Vladeck had also kept active in the field of Yiddish literature, reading all the significant writers and writing critical essays on many of them. He was also still composing Yiddish poetry, much of it on themes drawn from nature.[80] In 1917, in association with Kolya Teper and Leon Savitch, Vladeck edited a two-volume anthology of Yiddish writings on the general theme of social struggle, entitled "From the Depth of Our Hearts."[81] This collection was well regarded in Yiddish literary circles and may have been inspired by Upton Sinclair's famous English-language anthology, *The Cry for Justice*, which was published two years before.[82] Just as the Bund had been Vladeck's philosophical and political guide during his last years in Russia, so did the *Forverts* now serve as his spiritual and intellectual "home" in the United States. In combining "Yiddishkayt" with Americanization, his approach to the culture question was indistinguishable from that of the *Forward*. At times, his published views in this area simply echo positions taken earlier by Abraham Cahan as when Vladeck assented to the idea of a Jewish socialist saying Kaddish for a dead parent.[83] His political viewpoint, at least in its broad outlines, was also quite similar to that found in *Forverts* editorials, urging a strategy of practicality and moderation without formally repudiating the hope of revolution.[84]

As a veteran of the Bund, which had attempted to awaken the national consciousness of the Jewish people in Russia and Poland, Vladeck did not view patriotism as always and necessarily evil. Here again, the transition from the Bund to the *Forward* was readily made. Just as the *Forward* made a "socialist holiday" of July 4th, Vladeck paid tribute to the "stars and stripes," "The American flag," he wrote, "is just as much our flag as the red flag of the International. Both express living necessities, effective forces."[85]

In April, 1916, Vladeck was appointed City Editor of the *Forward* in New York City.[86] By this time, the Jewish labor movement had made great strides, especially in New York where the local branch of the United Hebrew Trades claimed a total membership of well over 200,000.[87] In 1914, Socialist Meyer London was elected to represent the Twelfth Congressional District on New York's Lower East Side in the House of Representatives. In the following year, another Socialist, Abraham I. Shiplacoff was elected to the State Assembly from a Brooklyn District. Both men were re-elected in 1916 when a third Socialist, Joseph Whitehorn, was elected to the Assembly from a Williamsburg district. All three legislators had been elected in districts made up predominantly of working-class Jews and in which the Jewish labor unions were strong and politically active.[88]

New York City socialism gathered additional momentum in 1917 from the two revolutions in Russia and from America's entry into World War I. The militantly anti-war stance of the Socialist Party[89] greatly enhanced its appeal in New York City where many, especially in the Irish, German and Jewish communities, remained for several months unreconciled to America's involvement in the war.[90] The party attempted to make the New York mayoral election a referendum on the war, nominating Morris Hillquit, the party's national secretary, for mayor on a platform combining opposition to the war with an extensive program of municipal reforms.[91] In the end, Hillquit obtained seventeen per cent of the vote, still the high-water mark for New York City socialism and the Socialists elected ten assemblymen, seven aldermen and a municipal judge.[92] Of the successful Socialist candidates, all but one were Jewish and, as in previous elections, each had triumphed in a largely Jewish district.[93]

During the campaign, in which he himself had been a candidate for alderman, Vladeck delivered speeches that implied, without actually saying so, that he opposed the war. In fact, his views on the subject were by no means those of his party. As early as December, 1915, Vladeck had been one of the few socialists to endorse the Preparedness Movement which would, he wrote, promote both "a just and scientific reconstruction of society and a healthy and intelligent working class."[94] His view of Preparedness was essentially the same as that expressed by such native-born radicals as Walter Lippmann and Charles Edward Russell and was shared by neither Abraham Cahan nor Meyer London.[95]

Vladeck was also critical of the principles upon which liberals and radicals were basing their hopes for a lasting peace. Thus, he criticized the resolution introduced by Congressman London against the annexation of territory on the ground that the Balkan question, which had led to the World War, would never be resolved without annexations.[96]

When the Zimmermann Note was made public by the American government on February 28, 1917, Vladeck wrote an editorial, stating that should the United States be attacked, all of its citizens would defend it "to the last drop of their blood."[97] Cahan endorsed the statement and made it the policy of the *Forward*, but it was denounced by Leon Trotsky and by the local New York branch of the Socialist Party.[98]

On Election Day, Vladeck easily carried the Fifty-sixth Aldermanic District in the Williamsburg section of Brooklyn receiving 2,802 votes to 2,023 for Harry Heyman, the joint nominee of the Republican and Democratic Parties.[99] During the next two years, Vladeck and the six other Socialist aldermen, who comprised a tiny minority of the Board, conscientiously pressed for action along a wide front. Scarcely any of the measures that they introduced, including bills for day-care centers, unions for municipal employees, public housing, and municipal ownership of streetcar and subway lines, were enacted.[100] In 1919, Vladeck was re-elected by a smaller margin, but the number of Socialists on the Board was reduced to four.[101] Two years later, aided by a partisan gerrymander of the district lines and by the split in the Socialist camp, the two major political parties defeated all the Socialist alderman.[102]

Although briefly in public office, Vladeck would continue to function primarily within the context of the Jewish labor movement. In September, 1918 he became manager of the *Forward*.[103] His first major involvement with the organized Jewish community came about during World War I in the movements to provide material assistance and moral support to the Jews of Eastern Europe. Vladeck was a leader in the People's Relief Movement that raised funds for the relief of Jewish war-sufferers in the tenements and workshops of the working class districts.[104] In 1919, Vladeck became a member of the administrative committee of the P.R.C. and in the following year he was one of five elected to represent it on the Joint Distribution Committee. The latter was the organization that disbursed in Europe the funds raised by the Jewish relief organizations in the United States.[105]

The leaders of the People's Relief were among the earliest advocates of supplementing, if not replacing, the original "palliative" relief programs of the "Joint" with the programs of reconstruction and retraining that were undertaken by it during the 1920's.[106]

Vladeck was also a major figure in the National Workmen's Committee, a movement organized in 1915 by Jewish socialists in the United States to agitate on behalf of equal rights for the Jews of Eastern Europe.[107] The N.W.C. was formed as the answer of the socialists to the Zionist-led campaign for an American Jewish Congress which was envisaged by its sponsors as a democratically elected representative body that would speak definitively for the whole of the Jewish community in the United States.[108] In opposing the Congress, which they viewed as nothing more than a vehicle for Zionist politics, the Jewish socialists aligned themselves with their natural foes, the upper-class Jews or "Yahudim." The latter were hostile to the proposed Congress, largely because it seemed to portend a militant Jewish nationalism in the United States which, if unchecked, might raise doubts about the ultimate loyalties of American Jews. Like the Socialists, many in the upper class elite deemed civil equality, but not "national" rights, to be essential for the Jews, whether in Eastern Europe or elsewhere.[109]

In the dealings that took place during the war between Jewish labor and the "uptown" elite, Vladeck had played a key role. By the 1920's, he became the main emissary of Jewish labor to other segments of the Jewish community, a position occupied earlier by Meyer London.[110] He now had the ear and the confidence of such figures as Herbert Lehman, Felix Warburg, and Louis Marshall. From these men and others of their class, he obtained financial contributions for causes with which he was in sympathy and intercession on behalf of individuals whom he was seeking to help.[111] With Marshall, who was a prominent lawyer and the president of the American Jewish Committee, Vladeck enjoyed a special relationship, corresponding with him on a wide variety of subjects, relating mainly to Jewish interests. At the height of the Red Scare in 1920, Marshall pleaded with Vladeck to dissuade Jewish radicals from demonstrating on Wall Street and elsewhere, lest they contribute to anti-Semitism which was already on the rise in the United States.[112] Two years later, Vladeck appealed to Marshall to intercede with the city on behalf of East Side pushcart peddlers who were being harassed by grafting policemen.[113] "I consider him." wrote Marshall concerning Vladeck in 1925, "a man of the highest character who has unselfishly devoted himself to the public welfare and whose influence for good cannot be exaggerated."[114]

Such collaboration across the boundaries of social class came naturally to Vladeck whose approach to socialism was thoroughly moderate and pragmatic. Although initially sympathetic, like virtually all socialists, to the Bolshevik regime in Russia, Vladeck opposed affiliation by the Socialist Party of America with the Soviet-controlled Third International.[115] Where the United States was concerned, he saw no real alternative to the lawful and accepted methods of democratic political practice.[116] "Revolutionary methods in a country not ready for revolution, he wrote in 1919, "can make only martyrs, not revolution"[117] The labor unrest of the postwar years led him to advocate not revolution but, like many socialists of this period, a political coalition among socialists, trade unionists and reformist liberals.

Moderate as his outlook was, Vladeck seems to have been in the mainstream of the Jewish labor and socialist movements. As we have seen, he played a lively role during the Revolution of 1905 in the Bund, the principle vehicle for Jewish socialism in Russia. After emigrating, he rose rapidly in the hierarchy of the *Jewish Daily Forward*, the main institution of the movement in the United States. The case for his representativeness is strengthened further by his leadership role in the 1920's and especially during the 1930's when he both founded and headed the Jewish Labor Committee and served as the leader of the American Labor Party bloc in the City Council of New York.[118]

Vladeck's continuing and growing prominence in the Jewish socialist movement suggests that the pattern of continuity and moderation that has been traced in this essay were not unique to him but characteristic of the institutions, such as the *Forward* and the Jewish unions, which comprised the movement's central core. Like Abraham Cahan, trade union leaders David Dubinsky and Sidney Hillman, Meyer London, and other moderate socialists, Vladeck was a quasi-assimilationist who accepted the Jewish workers as he found them while attempting to guide their adaptation to American life.[119] The full integration of the foreign-born would not be possible, he contended, without far-reaching social reform. "The problem of Americanization," wrote Vladeck in 1921, "is only a part of the general labor problem." Thus it was not only the foreigner that would have to be changed, "but America as well."[120]

In rising to leadership, Vladeck became not only a spokesman for, but also a symbol of, immigrant aspirations. This was demonstrated at his funeral on November 2, 1938 when 50,000 people gathered in the streets outside the Forward building on the lower East side of New York City to hear him eulogized by prominent figures, including Senator Wagner, Governor Lehman, and Mayor La Guardia. Thirty thousand people marched in the funeral procession through the streets of Lower Manhattan and across the Williamsburg Bridge, passing through the Brooklyn district that Vladeck had once represented in the Board of Alderman before concluding at the Mt. Carmel Cemetery in Queens. Tens of thousands (police estimates placed the total turnout at half a million) lined the streets and fire escapes along the line of march.[121] The size of the turnout, second only among Jewish working leaders to that at the funeral of Meyer London in 1926, demonstrated Vladeck's prominence among the group of "indigenous leaders" who, as Nathan Glazer has written, "symbolized (for the Jewish immigrants) the better world they sought."[122]

FOOTNOTES

[1]The most extended work on Vladeck is the author's dissertation, "The Early Life and Career of Baruch Charney Vladeck, 1886-1921: The Emergence of an Immigrant Spokesman." New York University, 1972. Good articles on Vladeck include John Herling, "Vladeck", *Survey-Graphic*, XXXVIII (November, 1939), 663-667, 700-701 and XXXIX (January, 1940), 29-31, 44-48 and Melech Epstein, *Profiles of Eleven* (Detroit: Wayne State University Press, 1965), Chapter Eleven.

[2]Daniel Bell, "Baruch Charney Vladeck," *Dictionary of American Biography*, XXII, 684.

[3]The name Vladeck was actually one of several pseudonyms that he used while a socialist agitator during the Revolution of 1905 in order to elude the Czarist authorities and it was not until he came to the United States that it became the name by which he was principally known. In 1915, he adopted it as his legal name upon becoming a citizen of the United States.

[4]The Pale, consisting of the Ukraine, Poland, Lithuania, and White Russia, was the westernmost portion of the Czarist Empire, to which nearly all of its Jews were confined by law.

[5]B. C. Vladeck, "Autobiography," unpublished m.s. in the Vladeck Papers, Part II, Box 7, Tamiment Library, New York University, typescript, 1-10.

[6]Three of the Charney sons became noted Yiddish writers. Samuel Charney (S. Niger), 1883-1955) the dean of Yiddish literary criticism, Vladeck, and Daniel Tcharney (1888-1959), a poet.

[7]Vladeck, "Autobiography," typescript, 22.

[8]Daniel Tcharney, *Dukor, memoren-ershter tayl* (Toronto: Tint und Feder, 1951), 60-66; Vladeck, "Autobiography," Pad I, page 4.

[9]"Autobiography," alternate chapter IV, (4-6), typescript, 14-16; See Paul Kellogg, "Gregory Gershuni, Schoolmaster-Terrorist," *Survey*, XVII (March 2, 1907), 1000-1004; Gershuni is referred to in Louis Greenberg, *The Jews in Russia* (New Haven: Yale University Press, 1951), Vol. II, 158-159.

[10]"Autobiography," Pad I, p. 9; Tcharney, *Dukor*, 266-267, 285-287.

[11]In addition to the persecutions of the regime and the flagrant anti-Semitism of the Russian and Polish peasantry, the Jews were also becoming steadily more impoverished due to the growth of their population and the gradual spread of the factory system in the cities of the Pale which displaced many Jewish artisans. See Salo Baron, *The Russian Jew Under Tsars and Soviet* (New York: Macmillan, 1964), 113-116 and Semen Dubnow, *History of the Jews in Russia and Poland* (Philadelphia: Jewish Publication Society, (1916-1920), III, 23-25.

[12]Greenberg, II, 181; Dubnow, III, 40-46.

[13]"Autobiography," alternate chapter IV, (7-8); Tcharney, *Dukor*, 267.

[14]In the Czarist Empire, the expression of heretical ideas was considered a crime and there were literally thousands of political prisoners in Russian prisons. See Sidney Harcave, *First Blood* (New York: Macmillan, 1964), 34.

[15]Daniel Tcharney, *Vilne* (Buenos Aires: Union Israelita Polaca, 1951), 74, 79; "Autobiography," typescript, 17-24.
[16]The quotation appears in Paul Sann, "Baruch Charney Vladeck," *Shelter*, III (December, 1938), 26.
[17]Moise Vilner (Baruch Charney, "A brif fun homel," *Folkzeitung*, Vilne May 4/17, 1906; Daniel Tcharney, *Vilne*, 76-80.
[18]"Autobiography, typescript, 41-43, 59-63.
[19]Meyer Weisgal, *So Far. An Autobiography* (New York: Random House, 1972), 4.
[20]Moise Vilner, (B. Charney) "Brif fun Poilen," *Folkzeitung*, Vilne, August 6/19, 1906.
[21]"Autobiography," Pad III, 68-71.
[22]"Tsu peretz's yohrtsayt," "*Jewish Daily Forward*, April 22, 1916; Tcharney, *Vilne*, 162.
[23]His 1908 writings include such essays as "Vi lukas bember hot geboyt a sukah," *Der Tog Ershaynt Oyf Shabes*, Vilne, No. 3, September 25, 1908 and "Hashanah rabbah manse," (Tale of the seventh day of Sukkoth), *Der Tog Ershaynt Oyf Shabes*, October 2, 1903. See A. L. Patkin, *The Russian-Jewish Labor Movement* (Milbourne: S. W. Cheshire, 1947), 143-144.
[24]Bonya Brokhes (Baruch Charney), "Vegen unser kultur problem," *Di Naye Tsayt*, Zamelbukh IV (1908), 83-88; Buntse Shvayg's eynikel (Baruch Charney), "Brif fun poylen," *Folkzeitung*, Vilne, August 6/19, 1906; See Irving Howe, *World of Our Fathers* (New York: Simon and Shuster, 1976), on Niger's views on Jewish culture. See Irving Howe, *World of Our Fathers* (New York: Simon and Shuster, 1976), 508.
[25]Bonye Brokhes, "Vos hert sikh in rusland," *Idishe Arbeiter Welt*" Chicago, December 18, 1908; microfilm Collection of the American Jewish Archives. "Autobiography," Pad III, 72-73.
[26]B. Vladeck, "Brif fun veg," *Der Tog Ershaynt Oyf Shabes*, Vilne, November 6/19, 1908; "Autobiography," Pad III, 77.
[27]Will Herberg, "The Jewish Labor Movement in the United States," *American Jewish Year Book* 5712, 1951, 1-15. J. S. Hertz, *Di yidishe sotsialistishe bavegung* (New York: Farlag Unser Tsayt, 1958), 92-94; Irving Howe, *World of Our Fathers*, 357-539; Moses Richin, *The Promised City* (New York: Corinth Books, 1964), 124-127.
[28]I will call him Vladeck from now on as this was the name by which he was chiefly known in the United States.
[29]*Idishe Arbeiter Welt*, Chicago, February 26, 1909 and December 3, 1909, Microfilm collection of the American Jewish Archives.
[30]Adolph Held, "Vladeck," *Der Fraynd* XXXIX (November, 1948). 5; "Autobiography," Pad III, 81.
[31]"Bibliografie fun B. Vladeck," in Ephim Jeshurin, *B. Vladeck, zayn leben un shafen* (New York: Forward Association, 1936), 433-436.
[32]B. C. Vladeck, "Grine un gele," *Idishe Arbeiter Velt*, Chicago, February 26, 1909.
[33]Hertz, op.cit., 92; Louis Levine, *The Women's Garment Workers' Union* (New York: B. W. Huebsch, 1924), 143; Matthew Josephson, *Sidney Hillman* (Garden City: Doubleday, 1946), 39.
[34]"Grine un gele;" "Autobiography," Pad III, 80-81.
[35]D. Shub, "Fun di amolige yohren," *Jewish Daily Forward*, March 14, 1965; *Idishe Arbeiter Welt*, Chicago, September 17, 1909.
[36]Hertz, op. cit., 115; Herman Frank, *A. S. Sachs, kempfer far folks-oyflebung* (New York: A. S. Sachs Society, 1945), "S-general" file, Vladeck Papers, Part I, Box 11.
[37]B. C. V., "A por verter," *Der Wecker*, New York, December 27, 1930.
[38]Levine, op. cit., 1955; *Jewish Daily Forward*, November 26 and 27, 1909; Elden La Mar: *The Clothing Workers of Philadelphia* (New York: Amalgamated Clothing Workers of America, 1940), 53; Matthew Josephson, *Sidney Hillman* (Garden City, L. I., 1946), 123-124.
[39]"Di idishe arbeiters un idishe unions in general strike in philadelphia," *Jewish Daily Forward*, March 11, 1910.
[40]"Di professionele bavegung in rusland," *Di Zukunft*, XIV (January, 1909), 28; B. V. (Vladeck), *Hundert finf un tsvantsig bilyon*," (pamphlet) (New York: Jewish Agitation Bureau, 1910), 41.
[41]Howe, op. cit., B. Vladeck, "A brif tsu a Bundist," *Idishe Arbeiter Welt*, Chicago, January 13, 1911, American Jewish Archives, Microfilm Collection.
[42]B. Vladeck, "Lomir Zikh lernen fun unser faynd," *Idishe Arbeiter Welt*, Chicago, October 28, 1910.
[43]"A brif tsu a Bundist."
[44]B. Vladeck, "Der arbeiter Ring in kontri," *Arbeiter Ring* (New York: Arbeiter Ring, 1910), 19-21.

[45] Howe, op. cit., 357.
[46] "Der arbeiter ring in kontn," 21.
[47] "Lomir sikh lernen fun unser faynd," Idishe Arbeiter Welt, Chicago, October 28, 1910; "Vos hert vikh in sotsialistishe amerika?," Jewish Daily Forward, December 10, 1911.
[48] B. Vladeck, "Di arbeiter ring in di groyse un kleyne shtet," Jewish Daily Forward, March 10, 1912.
[49] "Nit idishlokh nor sotsialistish tikhtig," Idishe Arbeiter Welt, Chicago, May 19, 1911.
[50] "Grine un gele," Idishe Arbeiter Welt, Chicago, February 26, 1909.
[51] "Autobiography," Pad III, 83-84; "Idishkayt un sotsialism," Part I, Jewish Daily Forward, June 26, 1911.
[52] "Vi azoi leben di iden in di south," Jewish Daily Forward, March 22, 1911.
[53] "Idishkayt un sotsialism," Part I, Jewish Daily Forward, June 26, 1911; "Autobiography," 84.
[54] This subject is discussed in Koppel Pinson, "Arkady Kremer, Vladimir Medem, and the Ideology of the Bund," Jewish Social Studies, VII (July, 1945), 234-260 and in Henry J. Tobias, The Bund in Russia (Stanford, California: Stanford University Press, 1972), 168-175, 274-276.
[55] "Idishkayt un sotsialism," Part I and II, Jewish Daily Forward June 26 and 27, 1911.
[56] "Vos es fehlt di idishe arbeiters in amerika," Jewish Daily Forward, May 22, 1911.
[57] "Di arbeiter ring in di groyse un kleyne shtet," Jewish Daily Forward, March 10, 1912.
[58] "Unser bavegung un das amerikaner leben," Jewish Daily Forward, September 7, 1911.
[59] "Vladeck — Early Correspondence," Vladeck Papers, Part II, Box 1 and 2; "Bibliography," in E. Jeshurin, B. Vladeck, in zayn leben un shafen.
[60] "Autobiography," Pad III, 85.
[61] Interviews with Steven Vladeck, December 9, 1970 and May Vladeck Bromberg, November, 1979; "Vladeck — Early Correspondence" and "Mrs. Vladeck — Early Correspondence" in Vladeck Papers, Part II, Box I. "Autobiography," Pad III, 85.
[62] J. S. Hertz, Di yidishe sotsialistishe bavegung in amerika (New York: "Der Wecker," 1954), 118-122; Will Herberg," "The Jewish Labor Movement . . . ," 25; Melech Epstein, Jewish Labor in U.S.A., (New York: Trade Union Sponsoring Committee, 1953), Vol. I, 350.
[63] Hertz, 141-142; Herberg, "The Jewish Labor Movement . . . ," 16, 25-26; Der Idisher Sozialist, New York, June 1, 1914; Di Naye Welt, New York, August 6, 1915.
[64] Telephone interview with Mrs. May Bromberg, May 7, 1970.
[65] "Sworn Statement of Baruch Charney Vladeck," March 3, 1937, "New York City" file, Vladeck Papers, Section I, Box 9; Charles C. Sava, Administrative Officer of the United States Department of Justice, to the writer, September 25, 1970.
[66] "University of Pennsylvania" file, Vladeck Papers, Section I, Box 12; Vladeck, "Autobiography," Pad III, 90-92.
[67] A.S. Sachs, Di geschikhte fun arbeiter ring (New York: Workmen's Circle, 1925), Vol. II, 500; B. Vladeck, "Der anfang fun der amerikaner literatur, "Di Zukunft, XXI (January and March 1916), reprinted in Jeshurin 401-418; B. Vladeck, "Bletlakh geshikhte fun tammany hall," Di Naye Welt, August 4, August 11, and August 18, 1916.
[68] Harold L. Meyers, Associate Historian of the Pennsylvania Bureau of Archives, to the writer, August 31, 1970.
[69] "Aseres hedibres far kempeyn-tuers, "Di Naye Welt, October 22, 1915.
[70] "A par personlikhe verter vegen a por sotsialistishe kandidaten," Jewish Daily Forward, October 31, 1918; "Algernon Lee iz der alderman velkher loyft itst far kongresman," Jewish Daily Forward, November 3, 1918.
[71] "Brivlakh tsu a fraynd," Di Naye Welt, February 11, 1916; See also "Di milkhume un preparedness," Jewish Daily Forward, December 10, 1915.
[72] "Brivlakh tsu a fraynd," Di Naye Welt, February 11, 1916.
[73] "Der bild fun karl marx," in Karl Marx, zayn leben, zayn virken, un zayne lehrer (New York: United Jewish Labor Organization, 1918), reprinted in Jeshurin, 300-303; "Fun der bukher velt," (a review of Ten Days that Shook the World by John Reed), Di Zukunft, XXXIV May 1919), 338-339.
[74] "Brivlakh tsu a fraynd," Di Naye Welt, February 4, 1916.
[75] Such figures as A. Litvak, M. Berman, and Dr. K. Fornberg were among those who returned to Russia after the revolution in March, 1917. Hertz, 163; M. Epstein, Jewish Labor in U.S.A., Vol. I, 63.
[76] "Brivlakh tsu a fraynd," Di Naye Welt, February 4, 1916.
[77] "Autobiography," typescript, 1, Pad I, 2.

[78]"Brivlakh tsu a fraynd," *Di Naye Welt*, February 4, 1916.
[79]"Natsionalism. Tsu der debate vegen natsionalism un di milkhume," *Jewish Daily Forward*, August 1, 1915.
[80]E. Jeshurin, *B. Vladeck in leben un shafen*, 55-88 and "Bibliography," 433.
[81]*Fun der tifenish fun unser hartz: a bukh fun leiden un kampf* (New York: Miller and Hellman, 1917).
[82]I. Kissin, "B. Vladeck's biografi," in E. Jeshurin, *op. cit.*, Interview with I. Rontsch, July 20, 1979; Upton Sinclair, *The Cry for Justice* (New York: Winston, 1915).
[83]"Fun mayn notitsbukh," *Di Zukunft*, XVII (August, 1912), 539-540. On Cahan's views, see Howe, *World of Our Fathers*, 112, 529 and Rischin, *The Promised City*, 133.
[84]See above, page 22. For Cahan's political views see Howe, 538 and Rischin, 159-160.
[85]Rischin, 167; B. Vladeck "'To Hell With the Flag,'" *Di Naye Welt*, April 14, 1916.
[86]Vladeck, "Autobiography," Pad III, 92-93.
[87]Frank Rosenblatt, "The United Hebrew Trades," *Jewish Communal Directory of New York City, 1917-1918* (New York: New York Kehillah, 1918), 1251.
[88]Mel Dubofsky, "The Success and Failure of Socialism in New York City," *Labor History* IX (October, 1968), 367-369; *New York Times*, November 5, 1914, November 3, 1915, November 10, 1916.
[89]James Weinstein, *The Decline of Socialism in America, 1912-1925* (New York: Monthly Review Press, 1967), 125-127; Nathan Fine, *Labor and Former Parties in the United States, 1828-1928* (New York: Rank School Press, 1928), 308-314.
[90]W. A. Swanberg, *Citizen Hearst* (New York: Bantam Books, 1963), 364-366.
[91]Weinstein, 145, 155; Fine, 322-323; *New York Times*, October 15, 1917. Paul H. Douglas, "The Socialist Vote in the Municipal Elections of 1917," *National Municipal Review*, VI (March, 1918), 132-133.
[92]*New York Times*, November 8, 1917; Fred Shannon, *The Socialist Party of America* (New York: Macmillan, 1955) 104-105; Weinstein, 154; Douglas, "The Socialist Vote . . . ," 138.
[93]Dubofsky, "The Success and Failure of Socialism . . . ," 370; Shannon, 105.
[94]"Di milkhume un preparedness," *Jewish Daily Forward*, December 10, 1915.
[95]"Brivlakh tsu a fraynd," *Di Naye Welt*, New York, December 10, 1915.
[96]*Ibid.*
[97]*Jewish Daily Forward*, March 1, 1917.
[98]Vladeck, "Autobiography," Pad III, 95-96; M. Epstein, *Jewish Labor in U.S.A.*, Vol. II, 76; Minute Book, Executive Committee, Local New York Branch of the Socialist Party, Tamiment Library, New York University.
[99]*New York Times*, November 8, 1917.
[100]Evans Clark "Legislative Tactics of the Socialist Aldermen," *New York Call*, May 29, 1919.
[101]*New York Call*, November 5, and 7, 1919; *New York Times*, December 3, 1919.
[102]*New York Times*, November 10, 1921; *New York Call*, November 10, 1921.
[103]*New York Call*, September 4, 1918; Vladeck, "Autobiography," Pad III, 101.
[104]Jewish People Relief Committee, *Di peoples relief fun amerika, fakten un dokumenten, 1915-1924* (New York: Special Book Committee of Peoples Relief, 1924), *passim*.
[105] *Ibid.*, 49, 64, 87; *Jewish Daily Forward*, November 14 and 15, 1920. "Joint Distribution Committee" file, Vladeck Papers, Part I, Box 7; Telephone interview with Mrs. Rose Klepfisz, Archivist of the J.D.C., July 15, 1971.
[106]Zosa Szajkowski, "Reconstruction vs. Palliative Relief in American Jewish Overseas Work," *Jewish Social Studies*, XXXII (Jan., 1970) 21-24.
[107]*Der Idisher Socialist*, New York, April 1, 1915; *Jewish Daily* Forward, April 5, 1915.
[108]Bernard G. Richards, "The American Jewish Congress," *Jewish Communal Directory of New York City, 1917-1918*, 384; Stephen Wise, *Challenging Years* (New York; Putnam, 1949), 203. Oscar Janowsky, *The Jews and Minority Rights, 1898-1919* (New York: Columbia University Press, 1935). 165-166.
[109]"Louis Marshall," *Universal Jewish Encyclopedia*, Vol. VIII, 382; Janowsky, 161, 168; Morton Rosenstock, *Louis Marshall, Defender of Jewish Rights*, (Detroit: Wayne State University Press, 1968), 52-54.
[110]London was the only Jewish labor figure among the original trustees of the Federation for the Support of Jewish Philanthropic Societies of the New York City; see *The Jewish Communal Register of New York City, 1917-1918*, 1254. He was also from the very outset involved at the highest levels in the raising of funds for Jewish War Relief. *New York Times*, October 26, 1914.

[111]"Herbert Lehman," file, "Louis Marshall" file, "Felix Warburg" file, all in the Vladeck Papers. Tamiment Library, New York University; Warburg, Marshall and David A. Brown Collections, American Jewish Archives, Hebrew Union College, Cincinnati, Ohio.

[112]Louis Marshall to Vladeck, October 13, 1920, Marshall Collection, Box 1590.

[113]Vladeck to Marshall, March 15, 1922, Marshall Collection, Box 64.

[114]Louis Marshall — To Whom It May Concern, May 5, 1925, Marshall Collection, Box 1597.

[115]B. Vladeck, "Against the Third International," *Socialist Review*, 59-61.

[116]B. Vladeck, "Vuhin zshe gehen mir?" *Jewish Daily Forward* February 21, 1919; "Against the Third International," 61-63.

[117]B. Vladeck, "Di amerikaner arbeiters un di amerikaner sotsialisten," *Di Zukunft XXV* (April, 1920) 215-216.

[118]John Herling, "Vladeck," Part II, *Survey Graphic*, XXXIX, (January, 1940), 48; Melech Epstein, *Profiles of Eleven*, (Detroit: Wayne State University Press, 1965) 341-342; 344.

[119]See the essays on the above leaders in M. Epstein, *Profiles of Eleven*; See also Will Herberg, "The Jewish Labor Movement in the United States," *American Jewish Year Book*, 5712, LIII (1951), 30-31, 65-66.

[120]B. Vladeck, "Americanization," (a review of the *Soul of an Immigrant*, by Constantine Pannunzio), Nation, CXIII (November 9, 1921), 541-542.

[121]The facts in this account of Vladeck's funeral are drawn from the stories in the New York press of November 2 and November 3, 1938.

[122]Nathan Glazer, "The Jews," in John Higham, (ed.), *Ethnic Leadership in America* (Baltimore: John Hopkins University Press, 1979), 23.

A Decade of Promise: General Eisenhower, European and American Jewry, and Israel, 1942-1952*

Ian J. Bickerton

General Dwight D. Eisenhower
(1890-1969)
U.S. Army Photo

There has been a significant transformation in the writing of the history of United States foreign relations in the past decade. The distinction between foreign and domestic affairs has all but been abandoned to be replaced by explorations of American policy as an expression or extension of the United States political economy. Any political economy has, of course, a cultural dimension, and ethnicity is the central feature of that cultural dimension in American life. There has also been a reawakened cultural awareness of ethnic identity in this country in the past decade and one result of this is that increasingly historians are exploring United States' relations with other countries in terms of ethnic identification and ethnic conflict. United States presidential policy towards Israel provides an interesting and important case to study the implications of this approach.

There are two types of questions suggested by this approach in the case of Israel. The first concerns United States policy toward Israel and American Jewry. In what ways, for example, did American Jewry attempt to influence United States policy? How successful were these efforts, and how can this be determined? Was this a good or bad thing — or to use the language of the political scientists — was it in the national interest? This leads on to a whole range of questions concerning the formulation of foreign policy, and what constitutes and who determines, the national interest which need not detain us here. The second set of questions, which should be answered before we can reach any satisfactory conclusions concerning the first, concern American Jewry itself. For example: what do we mean when we speak of American Jewry in this context — Zionists? non-Zionists? anti-Zionists? What was the relationship between the American Jewish community and the non-Jewish community in general, and especially in relationship to Israel? What was the impact of Israel upon the American Jewish community and non-Jewish community? Finally, and perhaps the most important question of all, to what extent were those active in seeking to influence United States policy and presidential attitudes aware of their success or failure?

Some of these questions and issues become clearer through a brief summary of what scholars and commentators have argued thus far. Concerning the first set of questions, i.e. those dealing with United States policy toward Israel and American Jewry, there has been a consensus on one aspect of United States policy, and quite bitter dispute on another. It has generally been agreed that United States policy during the Truman administration reflected the effective influence of the American Jewish community in securing a policy favorable toward Israel. Earl Huff and Alan Balboni, recent Ph.Ds who have explored Zionist influences upon United States foreign policy toward Palestine and Israel, for example, both conclude that the Zionist movement exercised a significant influence over the policies of the United States during Truman's presidency.[1]

There is also general agreement that United States policy toward Palestine and Israel, during the Truman administration, was formulated by the president and his advisers rather than by the State Department. As a result Zionists brought pressure to bear on the White House and Congress to counteract what was seen as the pro-Arab anti-Israel policies pursued by the State Department.[2] Thus, Huff concludes, American policy toward Palestine quite consistently parallelled the Zionist program during the period surrounding the birth of Israel. However, that very close parallel diminished markedly with the advent of the so-called "impartial" Middle East policy of the Eisenhower-Dulles era.[3]

Democratic party support for Israel is explained by several factors. American Jewry overwhelmingly supported the Democrats, and because of

Rabbi Abba Hillel Silver
(1893-1963)

their demographic concentration in a small number of key cities and states, they enjoyed an influence out of proportion to their numbers. The Democratic party was not only heavily dependent upon Jewish financial support, but drew upon the considerable influence out of proportion to their numbers. The Democratic party was not only heavily dependent upon Jewish financial support, but drew upon the considerable influence of American Jewry in such areas as the communications industry and the intellectual community. Richard Krickus in *Pursuing the American Dream: White Ethnics and the New Populism* summarizes these factors as follows: "It is indisputable that, vote for vote, no other ethnic group in American wields as much political power as the Jews do. Their political influence, of course, is not merely a function of their electoral strength which, with the exception of a few areas, is modest; the clout they wield is an extension of their economic prowess, professional talent, intellectual capability, cultural influence, and political acumen."[4] In view of all this it is not surprising, Krickus concludes, that Democratic party politicians were such staunch defenders of Israel.

It has also generally been agreed that the situation underwent significant change during the Eisenhower administration. American Jewry, it has been argued, lacked a strong power base in the Republican party, and had less access to the decision makers during the Eisenhower administration. Dwight D. Eisenhower has been described as being above politics: "Dad didn't like politics and he wasn't crazy about politicians,"

John Eisenhower recalled years later.[5] Eisenhower has thus been seen as free from, and able to withstand, political pressures because of his personal popularity. Eisenhower's military experience, plus the fact that he had not served in the House or Senate has led many, Zionist and non-Zionist alike, to conclude that he was not susceptible to Jewish political pressure. Of all recent presidents, writes Melvin Urofsky, Eisenhower "showed least inclination to befriend the Jewish community." Accordingly, Urofsky states, "the first five years of the Eisenhower administration marked the low point in relations between the Israeli and American governments."[6]

Alfred M. Lilienthal agrees. "The war time military leader," he writes of Eisenhower, "strove to steer the country on a neutral course in the Middle East, and away from the Truman blatant bias toward Israel." Speaking of events in 1956, Lilienthal observes "Ike proved to be the only American Chief Executive to stand firm against the full brunt of Zionist pressures when, in the fall of 1956, even though it was a national election year he refused to yield to political blackmail and sent his Secretary of State, John Foster Dulles, to the United Nations to halt the tri-pronged invasion of Egypt by Israel, Britain and France."[7] Emmanuel Neumann, president of the Zionist Organization of America, wrote of these years:

> In the United States we did not get much help or sympathy from the Eisenhower Administration which had come into office in 1953 'owing nothing to the Jews,' as some politicians put it. Its Middle Eastern policies were definitely shaped by the State Department, headed by John Foster Dulles, with its conglomerate following of Arabists, oilmen and missionaries. We had virtually no 'friends at court.'[8]

Several other factors contributed to Republican immunity from Jewish political pressure. According to Urofsky, "by the late 1950s, American Zionism as a movement had been rendered nearly impotent, a pale shadow of its once powerful self, with few members, little status and no purpose."[9] This led to a further weakening of Zionist influence upon United States policy makers. In addition, American Jewry harbored a deep seated hostility toward the Eisenhower administration because of the widely held belief that John Foster Dulles and Richard M. Nixon were anti-semitic. This confirmed the belief of American Jewry that the Republican party represented the WASP eastern establishment and followed policies unsympathetic to Israel.

Commentators do not agree, however, on whether or not Zionist influence was a good thing. Zionists, and many others among the Jewish community argue, not surprisingly, that their activities and American policy were in the national interest. Many other commentators however, including many in the State and Defense Departments, and I would venture to suggest that they are in a majority, believe just the opposite. To those who hold such views, Israel is the classic case in recent years of the determination of American foreign policy by domestic political considerations to the detriment of American interests. John Snetsinger, for example, in his study *Truman, the Jewish Vote and Israel*, concludes that "Truman's Palestine-Israel policy offers an extraordinary example of foreign policy conducted in line with short-range political expediency rather than long-range national goals."[10]

My own position is that all of the above conclusions are in need of revision or modification. In the first place, United States (more precisely, presidential) policy was not formulated in response to Jewish pressure to nearly the extent it has been claimed. Zionists claimed more credit than they deserve, and they were not as responsible for American policy as their critics believed. On those occasions when Zionist pressure appeared to be successful, it was largely because Zionist aspirations coincided with broadly based non-Zionist and non-Jewish attitudes. Furthermore, to the extent that Zionist/Jewish community pressure groups were successful in influencing American policy, it was just as effective in influencing Republican administrations as Democratic.

The Jewish community, increasingly bi-partisan in voting patterns in the 1950s, attempted in various ways, especially in presidential election years, to influence presidential policy favorably toward Israel. The Republican party, no less than the Democratic party responded to these overtures, but, like the Democratic party, in doing so did not modify substantially United States policy or goals in the Middle East. These goals involved many factors, including the United States need for Middle East oil, but they were not incompatible with support of Israel. Eisenhower inherited the problems and policies of the Truman administration concerning Israel, and the Middle East. These problems became visible very early. They concerned the settlement of the armistice truce lines, and border conflicts; Palestinian refugees; the status of Jerusalem; the Anglo-Egyptian controversy over the future of the Suez Canal zone and the Sudan; the growing dispute between Iran and Britain over the Anglo-Iranian Oil Company; economic, technical and military aid to the region; the need to protect and expand United States strategic and economic, especially oil, interests in the region; and, finally, although not least, the perceived need to keep the Soviet Union out of the area.

Eisenhower, despite the rhetoric to the contrary, pursued essentially the policies he inherited. Indeed, like his predecessor, he had few alternatives. The shift in policy which occurred during the Eisenhower administration was more apparent than real. As Abba Eban, then Israeli Ambassador to Washington, later reflected, the Eisenhower administration in 1953 was characterized by a "certain reluctance to confess that American policy anywhere was a continuation of what it was before. . . . Everything had either to be different, or one had to pretend it was different." Despite Dulles' moralistic and virtuous assertions "that American foreign policy would not be influenced by internal considerations, that the Arab interest would be upgraded, that Israel would be looked after, but downgraded ... nothing very much came of it in fact."[11]

At first glance it seems surprising that Eisenhower as president should be described as pursuing policies unsympathetic to Israel. After all, many Democrats, including perhaps even Truman himself, had hoped that Eisenhower might be the standard bearer of the Democratic party in 1952. But, more importantly, Eisenhower as the liberator of Europe had seen first hand the horror of the Nazi extermination camps. "Of all the distressing memories ... none will be sharper or more enduring than those of the DPs [Displaced Persons] and of the horror camps established by the Nazis," he wrote of this experience. "The Jews," he recalled, "were in the most deplorable conditions."[12] David Ben Gurion, who visited Eisenhower in October 1945 while touring the displaced persons camps, never forgot Eisenhower's "reaction of cold fury to the horrors of Nazism which unfolded before him when the forces under his command entered the concentration camps," and the compassion with which he set about rehabilitating the survivors.[13]

While commander of the American forces in Germany after the war, Eisenhower had been responsible for the administration of the displaced persons camps, and the setting up of separate Jewish centers or camps. He had assisted Jews fleeing from Poland, Roumania and Hungary into camps under his control, and aided the underground Jewish emigration from Germany to Palestine, despite British protests and State Department disapproval.[14] Following a six weeks' study of the conditions in the Jewish displaced persons centers in the American occupied zone in Germany in December 1945, the representatives of the American Jewish Conference (composed of sixty national Jewish organizations) had reported to Judge Simon Rifkind, Eisenhower's civilian adviser, "General Eisenhower's directives are superb, and the attitude of his staff has been excellent."[15]

Eisenhower, then, prior to 1953, had had considerable direct contact with the survivors of the Holocaust, and it might be thought that as president he would pursue a policy designed to sustain and support the state established to become their homeland. In any event, it is reasonable to assume that Eisenhower's war-time experience relating to North African Jews and his post war relations with Jewish displaced persons played an important role in shaping his later attitudes toward Israel and American Jewry. It is important, therefore, to examine Eisenhower's actions during the years 1942 to 1952 to ascertain as accurately as possible the attitudes toward Jews, Palestine, and Israel he displayed then, and which he later brought to the presidency. Such as examination reveals Eisenhower's behavior was a complex, and sometimes contradictory, mixture of compassion and humanitarian concern, and hard headed pragmatic political considerations. Throughout, first in dealing with discriminatory laws against Jews in Vichy French North Africa, then in his administration of Jewish displaced persons, and, finally, during the 1952 presidential campaign, Eisenhower's major concern appears to have been furthering his own career, and his political ambition. Rather than being above politics, Eisenhower during his army career developed a finely-tuned political awareness, which he used with great skill and subtlety in the years between 1945 and 1952 to further his career. In this context, he did not hesitate to draw upon the enormous reserve of good will and gratitude of American Jewry for his role as Allied Commander. "The Jewish people," he claimed in 1952, "couldn't have a better friend than me."[16]

II

In his memoirs, Eisenhower indicates that he had two contacts with the issues of the Middle East he was to face later as president. He first encountered what he described as "the age old antagonism between Arab and Jew" in the North African campaign in late 1942.[17] Prior to the allied invasion, local policy and Vichy rule had been to placate the Arabs by passing repressive anti-Jewish decrees, building concentration camps, and denying Jews civil liberties. The Arabs viewed the allied invasion with suspicion and regarded any attempt to ameliorate the condition of Jews as the beginning of an anti-Arab campaign. Eisenhower, in return for Vichy Commander-in-Chief Admiral Jean Francois Darlan's aid in obtaining a French ceasefire in French North Africa, agreed to a continuation of these policies. This "deal" with Darlan aroused considerable opposition in the United States and Britain, but Eisenhower defended the Darlan agreement on the grounds of "military expedience."[18]

Eisenhower's appointment of Marcel Peyrouton as governor of Algeria was even more controversial. Peyrouton as Minister of the Interior at Vichy had been head of the secret police, and had drawn up a code of anti-Semitic laws. Eisenhower's main concern, however, he wrote in his diary, was that Peyrouton was "an experienced administrator and God knows it's hard to find many of them among the French in Africa."[19] Eisenhower saw his decisions as "realistic" and was not only upset by criticism, but was frustrated by the time he had to devote to "difficult political manoever(s)."[20] He was also upset by the rumor that the "Jewish general" Eisenhower intended to set up Jewish rule in North Africa. Eisenhower did instruct the French authorities to relax the anti-Jewish laws and practices, but did not insist on immediate and total reversal because, he wrote later, he wanted to avoid Arab unrest or open rebellion behind the allied lines.[21] Even Rabbi Judah Nadich, the Chief Rabbi to the American Jewish forces in World War II and Eisenhower's first Jewish adviser following the war, recognized that "the rate of speed at which these changes were made might have been open to criticism," but he defended Eisenhower's policy as a prudent move to avoid setting back the military effort with the likely cost of "countless lives."[22]

This episode reveals a pattern of compassion tempered by shrewd political assessments which Eisenhower was to repeat in his handling of the displaced persons. Significantly, one of Eisenhower's first acts on encountering the Nazi death camps was to write to Chief of Staff General George C. Marshall urging him to send a delegation of Congressmen to confirm the existence, and conditions, of these camps.[23] Although Eisenhower did improve the condition of Jewish DP's, his assessment of the military and political realities was such that he was severely criticized in the United States for his failure to do more. He was sensitive to these attacks and bitterly resented them, as he believed the situation dictated that realism had to win out over idealism. His resentment was to increase in the months following the end of the war as a result of the report to Truman of Earl G. Harrison concerning the state of Jewish refugees in Europe.

In June 1945, at the suggestion of Henry Morganthau Jr., Secretary of the Treasury, Truman appointed Harrison, the American Delegate on the Intergovernmental Committee on Refugees in the State Department, to look into the future of the refugees, especially Jewish refugees, in Europe. This appointment was welcomed by members of the American Jewish community. Harrison was well known in Jewish and philanthropic circles for his work as Commissioner of Immigration and Naturalization Service in the Roosevelt administration. "I don't imagine there is another person in the country so universally beloved by aliens in the United States as he is," wrote Jewish social worker Jacob Billikopf to Charlie Ross, Truman's press secretary, of Harrison's appointment.[24] Executive Vice-Chairman of the United Jewish Appeal, Henry Montor, wrote to Billikopf that he was very hopeful about Harrison. "He struck me as being a tremendously sympathetic and alert person," he wrote, "he has it in his power to render a great service or obscure a great issue."[25]

Harrison was highly critical of the refugee situation he found in Europe. Harrison found that the military authorities refused to recognize Jews as a separate category or as stateless, despite their admitted greater suffering. He concluded that the policy of the military authorities was to treat all groups by nationality alone and to force repatriation by unpleasantness of surrounding and conditions. He urged that steps be taken to improve the billeting arrangements immediately, if necessary by requisitioning from the German civilian population, a step which the military authorities were reluctant to take. Harrison recommended that more camps for Jews be established on the model of the Feldafing camp, that UNRRA assume management of the camps as soon as possible, and that official assistance be given to relatives trying to trace their families.[26] On receipt of Harrison's report, in August 1945, Truman immediately sent a copy to Eisenhower stating that some of the conditions outlined needed prompt remedy. Truman acknowledged to Eisenhower that the task of meeting the needs of Jewish DP's was a huge one, and that conditions in some cases stemmed from subordinate officers not carrying out policies promulgated by Supreme Headquarters. The President urged Eisenhower to have his subordinates make more field visits, and to take whatever steps were appropriate to improve the housing conditions. It was essential, Truman wrote, to make clear to the German population that the United States thoroughly abhorred the Nazi policies of hatred and persecution.[27]

Eisenhower was angered and upset by Harrison's report. He wrote in *Crusade in Europe*, doubtless with Harrison in mind: "As usual, individuals with no responsibility in the matter [the treatment of displaced persons], their humanitarian impulses outraged by conditions that were frequently beyond help, began carrying to America tales of indifference, negligence, and callousness on the part of the troops. Generally these stories were lies."[28] His response to Harrison's report and its criticisms once more demonstrated that the level of his sympathy was determined by a keen political perception; he took steps to improve the situation, but at the same time he defended his previous relative inactivity. One of Eisenhower's first acts on learning of the report, the appointment of Judah Nadich as his special advisor on Jewish affairs, reflects his ambivalence towards Jewish DP's. According to Nadich himself, this is how the story unfolded. On August 7, 1945 Rabbi Steven S. Wise, President of the American Jewish Congress, cabled Eisenhower urging him to appoint a Liaison officer to his Headquarters to coordinate the activity of the Jewish DP's, and to help establish all-Jewish camps. Eisenhower replied to Wise on August 9 that he could not accept the proposal. Liaison officers, he stated, "are selected on nationality basis and it is considered undesirable on many grounds to have one specially for Jews."[29] The following day, August 10, however, Eisenhower received a cable from an anxious and troubled Secretary of War, Henry L. Stimson, requesting verification of the Harrison Report which concluded, "I want to emphasize importance we attach to this problem, and request that everything possible be done to improve present situation."[30] Eisenhower replied that he would immediately look into the entire matter. He seized upon the opportunity offered by Wise's suggestion, and, reversing his previous day's decision, appointed a special advisor. He did not let the occasion pass, however, without expressing the view to Stimson, which he later repeated to Truman, that "problems of this nature must not be oversimplified."[31]

On September 18, Eisenhower wrote a long letter to Truman outlining the steps he had taken to improve the conditions of the refugees and Jewish DPs in particular, vigorously defending himself against any suggestion of indifference or negligence. "As to the seriousness of the problem," he wrote Truman, "there is not the slightest doubt. The hopelessness of the ordinary displaced person comes about from fear of the future, which involves questions, always of international politics, and from the practical impossibility of participating, at this time, in any useful occupation." Eisenhower wrote of the Jewish DPs "I found that most want to go to Palestine. I note in your letter that you have already instituted action in the hope of making this possible." He pointedly added: "All of these matters are, of course, distinctly outside any military responsibility or authority and there is nothing whatsoever that I or my subordinates would be justified in promising or intimating in regard to them." Eisenhower was critical of Jewish DPs for their unwillingness to look upon "their present location as any form of permanent home." He explained to Truman that Germans were being thrown out of their houses to provide more and better accommodation for them; that DPs "camps" were not the old "horror" camps, and that every DP was in a "permanent building of some sort." He complained of a "distinct lack of cooperation" in one camp, and defended the army's behavior by reminding the President of the magnitude of the task to be carried out.[32]

In a second report, dated October 8, 1945, Eisenhower was even more emphatic in defending his policy, and it is clear that his perspective differed considerably from that of the DPs themselves and from that of the White House. Since Harrison's visit, the situation had improved markedly, Eisenhower asserted. Nevertheless, he added, "the housing problem must be seen in full perspective." There were a million and a half German air raid refugees and six hundred thousand Germans and others who fled before the advancing Red armies, as well as the troops and displaced persons to house. "Displaced persons had absolute preference over Germans for housing," but the needs of DPs were such that they were located in large installations such as barracks, apartment blocks and other public buildings in preference to scattered individual billets. On the recommendation of Rabbi Israel Goldstein, president of the United Jewish Appeal, Eisenhower had established exclusively Jewish centers and, he went on, Harrison's assertion that American military guards were "substituting for S S troops is definitely misleading."

Eisenhower admitted that there was room for improvement, and that "in certain instances we have fallen below standard." He assured Truman that he and the army would continue their real and honest efforts to meet the needs of the persecuted people, but he reminded the President "perfection never will be attained." Eisenhower concluded his report with an attack on Harrison:

> Mr. Harrison's report gives little regard to the problems faced, the real success attained in saving the lives of thousands of Jewish and other concentration camp victims and repatriating those who could and wished to be repatriated, and the progress made in two months to bring these unfortunates who remained under our jurisdiction from the depths of physical degeneration to a condition of health and essential comfort. I have personally been witness to the expressed gratitude of many of these people for these things.[33]

The depth of Eisenhower's resentment toward Harrison, and an indication of his awareness of American public opinion, and his political sensitivity to the damage adverse publicity could do to his reputation, can

General Eisenhower visits Nazi concentration camp near Gotha, Germany. April 12, 1945. U.S. Army Photo

be seen in a letter he wrote three weeks later to his mentor, George Marshall. "It seems to me that recently there has been a much calmer and better tone in the editorials and comments on the German and European situation," he wrote, "of course, it can blaze up at any minute because anything can happen. . . . Mr. Harrison is still shouting from the housetops to get Jews out of the centers in which we are taking care of them", he continued. "I wonder whether he knows that we are giving these people every ounce of food they eat, and how he would possibly distribute it if were had them scattered all over Germany."[34]

At the same time Eisenhower was privately expressing his anger at the criticisms levelled at him, he was publicly and actively reassuring Jewish DPs of his sympathy toward their plight, and his efforts on their behalf. On September 16, 1945 he visited the Jewish camp at Feldafing where he attended the Yom Kippur service. Eisenhower was enthusiastically applauded by his audience when he said: "We will do all possible to better the living conditions of those stilll residing in camps." The Commander in Chief instructed the congregation, however, to co-operate with, and to "obey all orders given by [the] military Government and the Army." He concluded, "my friends, it is my desire that you receive everything you deserve."[35] Eisenhower's visit to Feldafing, and the two other camps he visited that day, were widely reported and favorably commented upon by the Jewish press in America: "Not since Washington had addressed the Jews at Newport," ran the headline of the *American Hebrew*, of October 12, 1945, "had a general of the U.S. Army so addressed a Jewish congregation."[36] Nevertheless, Eisenhower was presented with two memoranda from camp Zionist groups vigorously protesting the overcrowded accommodation, the inadequate clothing and food, and restriction of movement at Feldafing, and, at the same time, requesting the General's help in having the doors of Palestine opened to Jewish immigration.

Despite the dissatisfaction of many of the DP's with the treatment they received at the hands of the U.S. Army, the political pressure from Washington, and his own sense of frustration and resentment, Eisenhower was so effective in improving conditions, and so successful in projecting his concern for Jewish DPs, that the *American Hebrew* awarded him their annual medal for the person judged "to have contributed most towards the promotion of better understanding between Christians and Jews in America."[37] Eisenhower was chosen for his record in Europe, "particularly in relationship to his attitude towards Jewish refugees, war prisoners and displaced persons." The *American Hebrew* particularly singled out Eisenhower's opening up of the concentration camps to the press and Congress which confirmed for many Americans, facts "so incredible they had inclined to doubt them."[38]

III

Following his departure from Europe to take up the post of Army Chief of Staff late in 1945, Eisenhower sought to maintain his favorable image with American Jewry. On February 4, 1946, for example, he presented to B'nai B'rith, on behalf of the Army, a citation praising the organization's contribution to the welfare of American sevicemen and women.[39] In February 1947 he addressed the National Conference of the United Jewish appeal which was launching a campaign to raise $170 million for the relief, rehabilitation and resettlement of the Jewish survivors in Europe. Stressing his role with the DP's he told those present; "Only one who has seen, as I have, the mental and physical effects of savagry, repression and bigotry upon the persecuted of Europe, can realize the full need for the material help and encouragement you propose to give.[40] Eisenhower's remarks as always, however, were carefully phrased, seemingly with a larger audience than American Jewry in mind, and he was studiously non-committal concerning the resettlement of the Jewish

DPs in Palestine, referring only to the United Nations indirectly, and then only as a machinery for disaster relief. His speech, although non-political in any partisan sense clearly, reminded American Jewry of their debt to him. The urgency of the situation in Europe could not be exaggerated, he said, and "acute disaster cannot await the functioning of vast machinery that has not, as yet, wholly emerged from the design stage." The U.J.A., through its charity, he added somewhat enigmatically "can do much to fill the breach." Eisenhower's address was used by the Jewish press to encourage contributions to U.J.A.[41] In August 1948 Eisenhower received further publicity in the Jewish press for his speech praising General Maurice Rose at the dedication of the hospital in Denver to honor the Jewish Major General who had commanded the 3rd Armored Division in Europe.[42] And in September 1948, while President of Columbia University, Eisenhower, upon the recommendation of Judge Rifkind, his former advisor on Jewish affairs in Europe, was awarded an honorary Doctorate of Humane Letters by the Jewish Theological Seminary of America, in New York. Eisenhower was described by the Chairman of the Seminary's board of overseers, Hebert H. Lehman, former Governor of New York, as a "beloved counsellor of our people in peace as in war."[43]

During the 1952 presidential campaign Eisenhower sought and received support from the American Jewish community. He was also sought out by Israeli leaders and American Jewish spokesmen for his views on the future of Israel and United States-Israeli relations. In February 1952, shortly after Eisenhower had told General Lucius Clay that he would be a candidate, Abba Eban and Moshe Sharett visited him at his NATO headquarters in Paris to discuss the problems confronting Israel, although Eisenhower was, it appears, non-committal.[44] Israel did not figure largely in the 1952 campaign, and at first Eisenhower moved cautiously in his public statements on this issue. He endorsed the Republican party platform which pledged continued "friendly interest" in Israel, of course, but he had little to do with drawing up the foreign policy plank.[45] When asked by a Tel Aviv daily newspaper, Haaretz, for a statement on Israel several weeks after the July Republican party convention, he refused. His campaign aide, Arthur H. Vandenberg, Jr., said that he would issue a definite statement when elected, adding that the friends of Israel would be pleased by Eisenhower's approach.[46]

Eisenhower did, however, issue a number of statements designed to gain Jewish support in the three months prior to the election. On August 28 he told Maxwell Abbell, President of the United Synagogue of America, that he was opposed to the provisions of the McCarran-Walter Act which discriminated against Jewish immigration to the United States, declaring, "The Jewish people couldn't have a better friend than me."[47] As election day approached, he increased his efforts to gain Jewish support. In mid-September he issued a long and warm statement of Rosh Hashonah greetings to American Jewry, which were well publicized and favorably

Abba Eban, ambassador of Israel, and Moshe Sharret, foreign minister of Israel, meet with President Eisenhower (1953). Courtesy of United Press International, New York

commented upon.[48] Eisenhower re-affirmed his goodwill towards "the spiritual descendants of Abraham" and he looked forward confidently, he said, to Israel's progress. "I have looked, and shall continue to look, with [a] sympathy to the state of Israel to achieve objectives vital to world peace and important to the future and destiny of the oppressed of the Jewish people." Eisenhower predicted "an ever firmer friendship," an enduring friendship, developing between American and Israel.[49] On October 14, Eisenhower issued an even more positive statement in support of Israel. At a dinner at the Waldorf Astoria hotel in honor of Senator Irving M. Ives arranged by the Greater New York Committee for State of Israel Bonds, Eisenhower's message stated that Israel was "democracy's outpost in the Middle East, and every American who loves liberty must join the effort to make secure forever the future of this newest member in the family of nations."[50]

A few days later, October 18, the National Republican Committee released an exchange of letters between Eisenhower and Abba Hillel Silver concerning Israel. In his letter to Silver, a staunch Republican, Eisenhower asserted that Republican support for Israel was not motivated by political expediency, but was based on genuine friendship and a belief in the inherent justice of the Jewish cause. It was in the interests of the United States to see that Israel survived and prospered, and Eisenhower declared his intention to do everything he could to establish peace between Israel and the Arab States. He reminded Silver that: "It will be one of the enduring satisfactions of my life that I was privileged to lead the forces of the free world which finally crushed the brutal regime of Hitler, with its responsibility for all those unspeakable atrocities." Clearly pointing to the obligation he believed American Jewry owed him, Eisenhower added: "Our forces saved the remnant of the Jewish people of Europe for a new life and a new hope in the reburn land of Israel."[51] Eisenhower and the Republican National Committee in the 1952 campaign, then, made extensive efforts to gain the support of American Jews.

The picture which emerges from this survey is that as Commander in Chief in Europe, and as Republican candidate for President, Eisenhower maintained a fine balance between sympathy and concern for European Jewry and Israel, and furthering his military and political career. There is no doubt that he was deeply distressed by the condition of the survivors of the death camps, but he did not allow his horror to override the other broad administrative and political considerations he faced in reconstructing Europe. He resented the criticisms directed at him concerning his handling of Jewish affairs, and although he gave way under pressure he asserted always the correctness of his position. Once he was sure of the personal benefits to be gained by the new course, he embraced it. When running for office, he did not hesitate to take credit for policies he had reluctantly been forced to follow as Commander in Chief when he believed it would gain Jewish votes. While he does not directly state as much, the evidence suggests that Eisenhower developed considerable hostility toward American Jewry because of the pressure they brought to bear upon him, directly and indirectly, and their demands upon him. He believed that American Jewry and Israel were under obligation to him, not he to them.

It was Eisenhower's ability to project himself as both practical, pragmatic and successful on the one hand, and as an idealistic man above politics on the other, which led him to be regarded as such a hero by the American people. Eisenhower revealed great political skill in the decade prior to his election. As Sherman Adams, his Chief of Staff wrote, "Although he had never held political office, his military experience had given him a considerable knowledge of government and government officials and the ways and means of getting things accomplished in Washington." Adams went on to say of Eisenhower, "actually he knew more about the intricacies of high government than many professional politicians, and had formed many firm convictions and beliefs about government and politics that were to weigh heavily on his later decisions."[52] Thus by constant reference to his war time role, Eisenhower skillfully sought to project himself as a friend of Israel. Yet throughout the period under review, Eisenhower remained ambivalent about the role he should play toward Jewish DPs, Israel, and American Jewry, and he attempted whenever possible to remain detached from the issues. He continued this pattern as President. It is interesting to speculate whether or not this would have been the case had he headed the Democratic party.

FOOTNOTES

*The author wishes to acknowledge with gratitude that research for this article was funded, in part, by the Lowenstein-Weiner Fellowship awarded by the American Jewish Archives, Hebrew Union College, Cincinnati, where much of the research was carried out.

[1] Alan R. Balboni, "A Study of the efforts of the American Zionists to influence the formulation and conduct of United Foreign policy during the Roosevelt, Truman and Eisenhower Administrations." (Ph.D., Brown University, 1973). Earl D. Huff, "Zionist influences upon U.S. foreign policy: A study of American policy toward the Middle East from the time of the struggle for Israel to the Sinai conflict." (Ph.D., University of Idaho, 1971).

[2] Zvi Ganin, *Truman, American Jewry and Israel, 1945-1948*, New York, 1979.

[3] Huff, "Zionist influences," p. 180.

[4] Richard Krickus, *Pursuing the American Dream: White Ethnics and the New Populism*, Bloomington, Ind., p. 207.

[5] Steve Neal, *The Eisenhowers: Reluctant Dynasty*, New York, 1978, p. 292.

[6] Melvin I. Urofsky, *We Are One! American Jewry and Israel*, New York, 1978, p. 305.

[7] Alfred M. Lilienthal, *The Zionist Connection: What Price Israel?*, New York, 1978, p. 535.

[8] Emmanuel Neumann, *In the Arena*, New York, 1976, p. 287.

[9] Urofsky, *We Are One*, p. 279.
[10] John Snetsinger, *Truman, the Jewish Vote and Israel*, Stanford, 1974, p. 140.
[11] Cited in Townsend Hoopes, *The Devil and John Foster Dulles*, Boston, 1973, p. 184.
[12] Dwight D. Eisenhower, *Crusade in Europe*, New York, 1948, pp. 467-8.
[13] Cited in Abba Eban, *Autobiography*, New York, 1977, p. 170.
[14] Judah Nadich, "Eisenhower and the Jews," *The Judean* (Canada) December, 1949, pp. 18-20, microfilm, "The Presidents and the Jews," American Jewish Archives, Hebrew Union College, Cincinnati, Ohio. (hereafter cited A.J.A.)
[15] Memorandum, American Jewish Conference to Judge Simon Rifkind, 13 December, 1945, Official File, Papers of Harry S. Truman, Harry S. Truman Library, Independence, Missouri. For a more detailed description of the role of the army see Leonard Dinnerstein, "The U.S. Army and the Jews: Policies Toward the Displaced Persons After World War II," *American Jewish History*, March, 1979, pp. 353-366.
[17] Eisenhower, *Crusade*, p. 136.
[18] Neal, *The Eisenhowers*, p. 134.
[19] *Ibid.*, p. 139.
[20] *Ibid.*, p. 139.
[21] Eisenhower, *Crusade*, pp. 136-137.
[22] Nadich, "Eisenhower and the Jews," p. 18.
[23] Alfred D. Chandler, Jr., ed., *The Papers of Dwight David Eisenhower*, Baltimore, 1970, Vol. IV, Eisenhower to Marshall, April 19, 1945, p. 2623. Eisenhower wrote to Marshall: "We continue to uncover German concentration camps for political prisoners in which conditions of indescribable horror prevail. I have visited one of these myself and I assure you that whatever has been printed on them to date has been understatement. If you would see any advantage in asking about a dozen leaders of congress and a dozen prominent editors to make a short visit to this theatre in a couple of B-54's, I will arrange to have them conducted to one of these places where the evidence of bestiality and cruelty is so overpowering as to leave no doubt in their minds about the normal practices of the Germans in these camps."
[24] Billikopf to Ross, June 29, 1945, Jacob Billikopf Papers, A.J.A.
[25] Montor to Billikopf, July 6, 1945, Billikopf Papers, A.J.A.
[26] Harrison Report, Dwight D. Eisenhower Library, Abilene, Kansas.
[27] Truman to Eisenhower, August 31, 1945 *Public Papers of the Presidents, 1945*, pp. 355-57.
[28] Eisenhower, *Crusade*, p. 467.
[29] Nadich, *Eisenhower and the Jews*, New York, 1953, p. 36.
[30] *Ibid*, p. 35.
[31] *Ibid*, p. 37.
[32] Eisenhower to Truman, September 18, 1945, Eisenhower Library.
[33] Eisenhower to Truman, October 8, 1945, Eisenhower Library.
[34] Eisenhower to Marshall, October 27, 1945, Eisenhower Library.
[35] Milton Marwil, "General 'Ike' at Feldafing," *The American Hebrew*, October 12, 1945, pp. 6-10, microfilm, "Presidents and the Jews," A.J.A.
[36] *Ibid.*
[37] *American Hebrew*, undated, microfilm, "Presidents," A.J.A.
[38] *Ibid.*
[39] "Remarks of General Eisenhower at presentation of citation to B'nai B'rith, microfilm, "Presidents," A.J.A.
[40] "Address by General of Army Dwight D. Eisenhower ... United Jewish Appeal," February 23, 1947, microfilm, "Presidents," A.J.A.
[41] Eisenhower's address was reprinted, for example, in *The Toledo Jewish Times*, November 7, 1947, to help reach the Toledo quota of $750,000, microfilm, "Presidents," A.J.A.
[42] *Intermountain Jewish News*, (Denver, Colorado), August 26, 1948, microfilm, "Presidents," A.J.A.
[43] "Seminary Honors General Eisenhower," undated and untitled, microfilm, "Presidents," A.J.A.
[44] Eban, *Autobiography*, p. 171
[45] Nadich, *Eisenhower*, p. 19.
[46] *Ibid.*, p. 19.
[47] *Intermountain Jewish News*, November 6, 1952, microfilm, "Presidents," A.J.A.
[48] Rosh Hashonah messages, 1952, microfilm, "Presidents," A.J.A. See cuttings from press.
[49] *Ibid*
[50] Nadich, *Eisenhower*, p. 20.

[51]*Ibid.*, p. 21. See also *Intermountain Jewish News,* November 6, 1952, microfilm "Presidents", A.J.A.
[52]Sherman Adams, *First Hand Report,* London, 1961, p. 27.

"Touch Life and You Will Find it Good": Charles Wessolowsky and the Southern Jewish Experience

Louis Schmier

Charles Wessolowsky
(1839-1904)
Courtesy of Louis Schmier

The mood was somber as the Jews of the 32nd Regiment Georgia Volunteers gathered outside Savannah at Battery Harris on September 6, 1862. They were meeting this Tuesday morning in protest against the expulsion of their fellow-Jews from Thomas County, Georgia, two weeks earlier.[1] The noise of their individual heated debates and discussions stilled as the meeting was called to order. One of the organizers of the meeting, Charles Wessolowsky, was called forward to speak. This twenty-two year old Private from Co. E was respected throughout the Regiment as one of the ablest and best educated men within the ranks. And while he was liked for his out-going personality and his wit, there was not to be any humor in his words or smile on his face this day. His words and gestures were sobered by a quiet anger at the action taken against those of his faith accused of profiteering.

The audience stilled as he lashed out against the citizens of Thomasville whom, he accused, would "clear their own skirts" by asserting their virtue of being American-born and who would use the foreign-born Jews as scapegoats to hide anyone from seeing "if they themselves don't partake of this extortion." With an unashamed pride in his heritage, Wessolowsky forcibly proclaimed that:

> as a people, willing as we were, and are, to struggle for our adopted country, to sacrifice all that is dear to us, to abandon our second home, and leave our wives and children to the care of strangers not belonging to our society, or fraternity, we, our armor buckled, enduring all toils and hardships of a camp life, ready to shed our blood for the defense of our country, now to be denounced, slandered and accused of unfidelity, and disloyalty to our country and government.

He then challenged "the gentlemen of Thomasville" to "see how many Jews and foreigners, more or less are in each (Georgia Regiments); ask them to peruse the lists of donations, and see how liberal and free-hearted the German Jews and foreigners are in behalf of aiding their adopted country."[2]

His listeners sat mesmerized by the force of these words. Morris Gortatowsky sat awed, thinking for a moment that he had just heard "Moses thundering down from the heights of Sinai with rebukes to the *goyim.*"[3] Under the same spell, the Jews passed a resolution which Wessolowsky helped draw up denouncing the "foul slander" as "unbecoming and unworthy of gentlemen" and calling for a boycott of Thomas County by all Jews.[4]

Tears filled Wessolowsky's eyes and his breath shortened as he watched the confident determination in the faces of his Jewish compatriots who came forward and signed their names to the resolution. Years later, he would recall this moment as one of the highlights of his life, for it had created in him the unshakeable belief that America was truly the bastion of religious liberty in which bigotry and persecution had no place and where the Jew could fearlessly combat them whenever and wherever they reared their ugly heads.[5]

Curiously, it had not been the pursuit for freedom of worship that had brought Charles Wessolowsky to American shores. Rather, it was escape from military service in the Prussian Army that led him to New York in 1858. He had immigrated from the village of Gollub located in the Prussian province of Posen where he had been born on September 3, 1839. His parents had become increasingly anxious as he approached conscription age. Their anxiety was heightened by the revocation of the rights that had been granted to them as Jews by the Prussian monarch during the tumultuous days of the Revolution of 1848. With disillusionment and resignation replacing their earlier optimistic expectations, and with their economic situation worsening, the future for their children did not seem at all promising. There was, however, a ray of hope. When Charles' older brother, Asa, had approached conscription age, his parents had faced an identical dilemma. Their decision was to send Asa to a relative who had earlier immigrated to the United States and who had settled down in a strange sounding place called Georgia. For about two years, they had been receiving letters from Asa in which he never stopped glorifying his newly-adopted country as a land of opportunity and freedom. One of Asa's latest letters had contained the suggestion that Charles be sent to him. The Wessolowskys hesitated in following Asa's advice because his letters also had contained news that he had become somewhat lax in the ritual observance of Judaism. Circumstances, however, offered no alternative choice for Charles. And so, with a little traveling money in his pocket, a few pieces of clothing in his hand-pack and a parental benediction in his heart, he set off for America. During the lonely hours at sea he kept thinking of the urging of his parents that he should never forsake the faith of his forefathers; that while he should learn to act as an American and speak as an American, he should never stop being a Jew in America.[6]

Immediately upon landing in New York, the young Charles headed South. He rode the train as far as what little money he had would take him. From Richmond he walked to Sandersville, the county-seat of Washington County in northeast Georgia. If Charles was expecting a respite upon his arrival in Sandersville, he was disappointed. It seemed to him, when reflecting in his later years of these moments, that as his brother took his travel pack with one hand he gave Charles a peddler's back-pack with the other. Charles, however, resisted his brother's order to start peddling the countryside the day after he had arrived on foot in Sandersville. Not only was he exhausted, but he sharply reminded his brother that it was the Sabbath. Older brother or not, Charles proceeded to reprimand his brother for ignoring the teachings of *cheder* and the traditions of their home. His call upon religious conviction to stay in Sandersville was due, as he later admitted, to a quest for an excuse to hide his fears rather than a reason against venturing out into the countryside alone. Morris Gortatowsky's daughter remembers how he would laughingly remark how foolish he was in his younger days to have held such fears. To the newly arrived eighteen year old Charles, however, such fears were very real. Only when his brother virtually pushed him out through the door on the following Monday did he dare accept his brother's promises that he would be safe.

"Uncle Charles would always laugh as he described himself and how he felt on that first peddling trip," warmly recalled Sadie Gortatowsky Davis. "There he'd be with his 'store between his shoulders — that's what he called his peddler's pack — loaded with threads, needles, buttons, pieces goods and other things. He didn't know the language or how to count in American money. He didn't know where he was or where he was going. All his brother did was to point him in a direction, give a shove and say firmly 'Geh!' He was isolated and alone among the trees, the wildest animals he could imagine and the *goys*. He'd give the loudest laugh as he said he didn't know of which to be the most frightened, the bears his brother warned him about or the first farmer he'd meet."

To his surprise and his relief, on this trip and on all succeeding trips, he did not meet any devouring bears; nor did he meet any devouring Gentiles. Instead, he found that the rural farmers displayed characteristics he did not know existed in the Gentile personality. The Georgia Gentiles were a different breed of Gentile from his family's bigoted neighbors in Gollub. He would never have thought a Jew could experience the warmth and friendliness with which he was received in the homes of his Gentile customers. He was "stunned and speechless" the first time one of his customers asked him to eat with his family and spend the night in his house during a violent rainstorm.

"The first meal Uncle Charles ever had in one of those farm houses was a slab of bacon," smirked Mrs. Davis. "He liked to died. He ate it, choking on every bit and swallow, as he used to tell us over and over. But, he ate it because he was afraid not to and upset his hosts. He didn't know what they would do if he refused their hospitality. He stayed up all that night praying and asking for forgiveness. You know, he never could, as I recollect, eat that stuff." Soon, however, after a number of peddling trips the farmers learned what the young boy could eat as he nervously began to ask for dairy meals and then went out of their way to provide him with acceptable foods. Their respect for his religious observances made quite an impression on Charles. That a "Jew-hating" Gentile should display such toleration towards a "Christ-killing" Jew, seemed to indicate to Charles that personal relationships and displays of honesty were important in overcoming generations of culturally bred fear, suspicion and hate.[7]

Charles returned from that first peddling trip somewhat dazed. Not only were the farmers congenial, but they were grateful and helpful as well. They did not take advantage of his ignorance of the language and did not cheat him. He had to admit that his brother was right that all would be safe if he avoided the bears. He would soon come to think, however, that his brother was wrong in abandoning all attempts at keeping to religious observance as a means of eliminating outward differences from the Gentiles and insuring safety among them. The reception he had received and the respect accorded him on later trips would lead him to the firm conviction that he would not have to survive in America, or become integrated into it, at the sacrifice of his religious devotion and practice. In the months and years to come, he would argue with his brother and friends that the choice offered the Jew in Gentile America was not one of complete assimilation or isolation. Rather, an accommodation could be reached whereby the Jew could become an American socially, politically and nationally and remain a Jew religiously, morally and ethically. In fact, he would argue in decades to come that the ethical heritage of the Jew makes him a superior American citizen who gives to his country more than he takes because of this instinctive dislike "to share the public charity" and his moral virtue that renders all law enforcement agencies unnecessary.[8]

It was within a few months after his arrival that Charles decided he could become a part of this new land rather than remain apart from it. His brother's means were too negative for his outgoing personality. Safety in distance and conformity was not suitable to his independent outlook. At the same time, his extensive educational training provided him a framework of discipline wherein he could learn both the language and culture of the land in which he was living.

He found the farmers were more than happy to help him learn English. "He once said," remarked Mrs. David, "he always felt the country folk thought if they couldn't convert him to their religion they could at least change his ways." While the parents would teach him the individual words for the various commodities he was selling, the children took out their primers and taught him how to read. "Uncle Charles used to say," Mrs. Davis continued, "that the children got a kick out of being a teacher rather than a student. They used to play 'school' with him and even scolded him if he didn't mind their orders."[9] It was not long before Charles was packing a primer of his own in his back-pack. Throughout the trip he would read to himself, struggling through the pages. He read the primer at every opportunity: while he was walking between farms which caused him many a bruise as he fell over stone, sticks and ground depressions; while he was resting; just before he went to sleep. In fact, the primer became his second prayer book, for whenever he read from his prayer book he would immediately read for at least five minutes from his primer. After the primer he graduated to reading literary classics. He would read these works aloud trying to eliminate his accent and speak like the natives.[10]

In early 1859, Asa took on his brother as an equal partner in their newly-formed "company" that they established a few miles east of Sandersville in Riddleville. The "company of two," as one observer described it, was little more than a crude device designed to secure additional credit from the Savannah merchant houses.[11] On one of these credit-seeking trips to Savannah, Asa arranged a marriage for Charles. After all terms had been agreed upon, on March 24, 1859, Charles married Johanna Paiser.[12] Morris, the first of three children, was born a little more than nine months later in Riddleville on January 1, 1860.[13]

With the added responsibility of supporting a family, Charles convinced his brother it was time to strike out for greener pastures. In early 1861, the Wessolowsky brothers closed their Riddleville shop and headed for Savannah.[14] Whatever long-range plans Charles might have had for the future, they were altered with the bombardment of Fort Sumter.

On May 7, 1862, Charles, who had been sent to this country to avoid military service, enlisted along with his brother as a Private in Co. G, 57th Regiment Georgia Volunteers. The unit was quickly reorganized as Co. E, 32nd Regiment Georgia Volunteers and assigned to garrison duty in the Savannah area.

Immediately after the incident at Thomasville, the Regiment was moved north for garrison duty at Charleston, S.C. For the next two years, Wessolowsky fought in minor engagements as his unit was moved up and down the East Coast protecting the Atlantic ports of Jacksonville, Savannah and Charleston.[15] During this period, in recognition of his leadership qualities, Wessolowsky was promoted to Sargeant-Major. It was another lesson for this young Jew about the rewards of becoming part of an hitherto alien Gentile world without having to renounce his heritage and faith. On November 28, 1864, his military career came to an end. His Regiment had been moved from Charleston to Marietta, Georgia, as part of the force defending Atlanta. In a skirmish at New Hope Church in Dallas, Georgia, a few miles southwest of Marietta, Wessolowsky was captured. He spent what remained of the war at Hilton Head prison.[16]

At the close of the war, he returned with his family to Sandersville. The destruction wrought by Sherman's troops to the area and the lack of available goods, however, made it impossible to start a business.[17] By the beginning of 1866, Wessolowsky was back in Savannah operating a small general store with his brother.[18] His knack for business, however, could never reach the heights of his skill with words. Despite a growing post-war boom, he was unable to stave off his creditors. Leaving his brother in Savannah, he traveled 120 miles west to Albany, Georgia, lured there by promises of success offered by his cousin, Adolph Kieve, and an old comrade-in-arms, Morris Gortatowsky.[19]

Unfortunately, Wessolowsky did not leave behind in Savannah what was judged "his poor practice for money."[20] He went into partnership with one of the local Jewish merchants. And though the business thrived for about eighteen months, it eventually failed under circumstances, as one observer noted, "that smacked of fraud."[21]

Apparently his limited economic success and a general recognition that he was without any business sense, had little effect on the extent of the social and political position he was to achieve in Albany.[22] For though his friendliness, wit and charm were likeable traits to both Jew and Gentile, it was his learning, his leadership qualities, and his willingness to become involved in civic affairs that forced Albanyans to ignore the defects in his commercial character.

Almost from the moment of his arrival in Albany, the thirty Jewish families agreed he should be their leader. His extensive Biblical and Talmudic training, his fluency in Hebrew, his knowledge of ritual and ceremony and his oratorical ability were credentials they could not ignore.[23] For his part, Wessolowsky accepted this position within Albany's

Jewish community because as he was to write later: "the golden calf alone does not constitute the happiness of man, and that religion in its pure and untarnished state, with its teaching of morality and truthfulness, is also essential and requisite for the unalloyed pleasure and felicity of this world."[24] For the next twenty-three years, until the Jewish community acquired the services of an ordained rabbi, Charles Wessolowsky performed all the services demanded of a religious leader. He led the religious services during both the Sabbath and holidays, performed burials, presided over marriages, consecrated cemeteries and dedicated temples.[25] At times, in conjunction with his peddling trips, he acted as a circuit-rabbi performing similar services for Jews living in towns along his route.[26]

In addition, as patriarch of the Albany Hebrew Congregation he felt obliged to insist that his fellow-Jews perform their social duty as prescribed by Jewish law. Under his guidance, the congregation formed a Hebrew Benevolent Society for the purpose of distributing charity to the needy. Always looking to the future, Wessolowsky organized a Sabbath school in which he provided the religious and moral training of the children which he felt was so vital if Judaism was to survive.[27]

Wessolowsky's zeal was not confined solely to serving the religious and moral needs of Albany's Jews. Haunted by the ghosts of Thomasville and drawing upon his personal experiences, he felt it essential that the Jewish community earn the respect of the Gentiles and demonstrate to them that the Jews can contribute to the vitality and stability of the town. And while a few of the Jews were already active in civic affairs, none displayed his energy and enthusiasm. "He sometimes felt as if he alone could bring Jew and Gentile together by presenting himself as a representative of all of what a Jewish citizen truly was. And he succeeded in showing that the Jews could help the town if given a chance," explained Mrs. Davis. He always refused to be hindered by any possible negative reaction that might result from such attempts to be involved. Indeed, he was prone to lay the blame for such adverse reaction at the feet of the Jews themselves. To his way of thinking, it was their responsibility to stand up and claim what was rightly theirs as guaranteed by law; it was their responsibility to demonstrate to the Gentile majority that they did not threaten the stability of society; it was their responsibility to earn the respect of the Gentiles; and it was their responsibility to educate the Gentiles in Jewish ways; and finally, it was their responsibility to eliminate the source of ignorance in which breeds suspicion, fear and hatred. "He once said he felt like a Jewish missionary among the Gentiles to show the way for other Jews."[28]

The citizens of Albany began to feel the effects of Wessolowsky's "mission" almost the moment he arrived in town. The point of his initial contact was Albany Masonic Lodge #24 and later Albany Chapter #15 Royal Arch Masons.[29] The members of these lodges, who included the most prominent citizens of the town, quickly came under the same spell that he cast over anyone with whom he came into contact. That spell would translate itself into a respect, admiration and even a near-reverence. The road to such a position of dignity in the community, which was certainly aided by a glowing war record, had humble beginnings.

In 1869, he volunteered to be a floor manager of the Lodge's annual Calico Ball.[30] The efficiency with which he organized and managed the Ball made quite an impression within the lodge. Not wishing to let a man with his abilities remain idle in their midst, the membership elected him to an office. The reaction of the Lodge soon spilled over into the political activities of the town. The leaders of Albany felt Wessolowsky, regardless of his faith, had something to offer the town. At the end of 1869, they convinced him to run for Alderman on A.C. Westbrook's "working man ticket."[31] Though he was not elected, the absence of any anti-semetic comments during the campaign led him to believe he should try again in the immediate future. It was a curious decision for a man who would later promote the image that the Jew was rarely involved in politics because of the time demanded of his commercial enterprises the income from which he could use to be a better citizen.[32] Nevertheless, in 1870, in spite of business difficulties, he ran successfully for alderman. His political career continued when, from 1871 to 1875, he held the position of Clerk of the Superior Court of Dougherty County. He was elected next to a two year term as State Representative which was followed by a one year term as State Senator. He was the only Jew to have held all these elected offices.[33] There was even some discussion in political circles at the end of 1877 about nominating him for the United States Senate. That idea, however, proved to be too radical and nothing came of it.[34] Nevertheless, Wessolowsky had opened the way in Albany for other Jews to follow. For the next fifty-five years, it was axiomatic that a leader of the Jewish community sit on the Board of Alderman and later on the City Council.[35]

During the session of the state legislature in 1875, Wessolowsky attended a lecture given by Rabbi Edward B. Browne on the ethics of the Talmud. The two met after the presentation and discussed its contents. Browne left Atlanta impressed not only that he had discovered a Jewish state representative who was "honoring Judaism," but one who was so learned in Talmudic law. What seemed at the time as little more than a passing conversation took on greater importance when, in 1877, Browne was elected Rabbi of the Hebrew Benevolent Congregation in Atlanta.

Immediately after assuming his position, Browne prepared for the publication of a weekly he called *The Jewish South*. It was to be the region's first Jewish newspaper. Because of the demands of his pulpit responsibilities and a myriad of other activities in which he was involved, Browne was looking for an associate editor who could assume the duties of editing the paper whenever necessary. His choice was almost preordained, for no matter from whom he sought advice and help in his search for an assistant, Wessolowsky's name was always mentioned. Aside from general character references, Browne was particularly impressed when told that Wessolowsky would regularly endure the difficult trip back to Albany to perform his duties as patriarch of the Albany Jewish Congregation.[36] Equally impressive — and important — to Browne was Wessolowsky's growing involvement with B'nai B'rith.

Wessolowsky's first experience with B'nai B'rith occurred in Savannah where he joined Joseph Lodge, No. 76, in 1866 and rose to the position of Vice-President.[37] At first, the Lodge meant little more to him than a meeting place for Jews searching out the comfort of associating with their own kind. His attitude changed, however, after joining the Masonic Lodge in Albany. The sense of unity and cameradere generated not only within the Lodge but between Lodges in different towns indicated to Wessolowsky that the B'nai B'rith could serve a similar and sorely needed function among the widely scattered Jews.[38] Upon his arrival in Atlanta in 1875, Wessolowsky realized that the dispersal of the Jews throughout the land was not the only problem that threatened a sense of Jewish unity. For during this period, the Jews were experiencing religious division as rituals and ceremonies underwent examination, ancient doctrines were questioned, prayer books were revised, and traditional observances and practices were re-evaluated. The ensuing debates and opposing positions, which at that time were unknown in Albany but which were active in Atlanta, were those associated with the attempts of American Jews to decide whether to move from traditional Judaism to reform and if so, to what extent. Wessolowsky was personally confronted with the issues that were replacing Jewish unity with a disjointed mosaic. He saw B'nai B'rith, with its emphasis in advancing the rights of Jews and promoting both cultural and educational activities, as a unifying institution in which Jews could practice their traditional moral and ethical responsibilities without touching upon the sensitive and divisive religious issues.[39]

Browne was sympathetic to Wessolowsky's deep concern with the need to re-establish a sense of brotherhood among Southern Jews. Moreover, Wessolowsky's activities had some very practical considerations, for having become active in the promotion of the ideals of B'nai B'rith Wessolowsky was about to be elected to a high position in the Grand Lodge of District No. 5.[40] As such, his renown and subsequent contacts throughout both the 5th District and the South could prove useful to the promotion of Browne and his *Jewish South*.

With all these factors in mind, Browne offered the associate editorship to Wessolowsky. Even though his term as State Senator was about to end, Wessolowsky was hesitant about accepting Browne's proposition. Browne was the religious leader of the Reform-leaning Hebrew Benevolent Congregation. And though Wessolowsky was not close-minded about the needs for possible change in the worship of Judaism, he was not committed to the Reform movement. He advised Browne that he would not consider a position with *The Jewish South* if it was being designed as a periodical preaching Reform Judaism. Wessolowsky underlined his fear by pointing out that since Browne was a protegé of Isaac Mayer Wise, the founder of the American Reform movement, he wanted specific assurances that *The Jewish South* would not be a mere regional organ of Wise's *Israelite*.

Browne assured Wessolowsky that he would "stand fearless and independent" and would not champion one form of Judaism over another. Among the aims of the newspaper, Browne explained, involvement in the sensitive liturgical and theological arenas was not included. As Browne ran down the list of purposes he had set down for the newspaper, Wessolowsky perked up: the periodical would be an educational instrument attempting to heighten the cultural awareness of Southern Jews; articles would be printed specifically designed to increase the basic religious knowledge of its readers; it would be a clearing house for news about the activities of Jews and Jewish communities in the South; it would create a news network of events of particular interest to Southern Jews; as a Southern-based and Southern-oriented newspaper, it would be free of the "Northern" perspectives emanating from Cincinnati, Philadelphia and New York; it would be an instrument of unity promoting by whatever means possible a sense of common interest and finding a common ground on which all Jews, regardless of their religious position, could stand together; it would promote a sense of Jewish brotherhood by emphasizing the activities of fraternal lodges; and finally, it would inform the Gentiles of Jewish ways and thereby hopefully drain the swamp of ignorance in which bred all diseases of bigotry.[41]

With an unsure political future and little economic prospects, Wessolowsky accepted Browne's offer.[42] For the next four years, until his departure in 1881, Wessolowsky served as Associate Editor of *The Jewish South*. The newspaper provided him a vehicle with which he could travel to Southern cities, towns, villages, hamlets and crossroads promoting not just the newspaper or even B'nai B'rith. More important to him, he could promote his three watchwords: pride, unity, conciliation.[43]

In his capacity as Associate Editor of *The Jewish South* and as a leading figure in Southern B'nai B'rith activities, he was in constant demand as a speaker. Wherever he went he observed and commented on the status of the Jews within both their own community and that of the area as a whole. The criteria and standards by which he judged the Jews he met were the same values by which he lived and the same demands he made of himself. He took great pride in the economic success of his fellow-Jews throughout the South. The size and number of the Jewish mercantile establishments was for him a sign of the successful transplantation of the immigrant Jew into the economic soil of the South. He was particularly moved as he observed the Jewish plantation owners in Louisiana and Mississippi. He saw them and their agricultural activities as evidence of a reawakening of the desire among Jews to return to the traditional and Biblical labors of their forefathers.[44] Moreover, the existence of "Jewish farmers" was further evidence that the United States was truly a bastion of liberty in which there was no room for prohibitions against the Jews owning land.

The success in finding a livelihood for the Jew in America was dependent largely on his cultural adjustment. For this reason, any cultural activity in any of these communities was noted with great exhaltation. He saw in the balls, the dances, the recitals, the plays the signs that the Jews never ceased to cultivate their spirit no matter how arduous the struggle to become a part of Gentile society.

His pride in economic success and respect for cultural achievement were muted if such accomplishments were not utilized to augment the religious life of the Jewish community. Wessolowsky reserved his greatest applause and most caustic comments as he observed the religious activity of the Southern Jewish communities. Wherever he traveled, he looked for the watchtowers of his faith: a synagogue in which the community worshipped; a Hebrew Benevolent Society or Ladies Aid Society through which the community carried out its charitable responsibilities; a fraternal lodge with which a sense of brotherhood was forged; and a Sunday School in which the future of Judaism, the children, were educated in the ways of their faith. The decibel level of his applause was proportional not only to the existence of these institutions, but according to their activity in promoting what Wessolowsky called the "cause of Judaism." "They boast of a temple," he wrote of the Jews in Monroe, Louisiana, "but *of what avail?* ... the temple stands, magnificent in its structure, grand in its appearance, until the time arrives when our co-religionists, either for fear, or habit and custom see fit, at least, to keep three holy days in the year."[45]

Conversely, his applause for the existence and operation of some of these institutions in a community was balanced by quiet admonishments in the absence of some. He heaped all kinds of praise on those few communities which displayed all the "proper" characteristics and contained all the necessary organizations. His anger boiled up, however, in those communities where the Jewish religious structures, social organizations and fraternal lodges were not to be found. He chastised them for their assimilationist tendencies, and vigorously condemned their disdainment for their heritage, their disinterest in following their faith and their disinclination to train and educate their children in ways of Judaism.

Upon his return to Albany in 1881, Wessolowsky engaged in a series of mediocre business ventures until he went into partnership with his son.[46] Never a merchant at heart, Wessolowsky directed his energies in other areas. He immediately took up once again his position as patriarch of the Albany Hebrew Congregation. It was largely through his personal efforts that the Congregation built its first synagogue in 1882 and its second in 1896. Not only did he serve as a continuous member of the Congregation's Board of Directors, but served as its President from 1889 until 1894.[47]

If he continued to foster an active religious life in the Jewish community, he also renewed his "mission to the Gentiles." Though he did not engage again in political activities, he devoted himself to serving the Masonic Lodge. From 1895 to 1897, he held the lofty position of Grand High Priest of the Grand Chapter of Georgia, Royal Arch Masons, and from 1897 to 1898 was Worshipful Master of Masonic Albany Lodge #24.[48]

Interspersed with the demands imposed on his time and energy by his congregational and Lodge activities, Wessolowsky lectured throughout the South promoting the cause of the Masons, B'nai B'rith and Jewish-Gentile relations. During one such lecture in Tampla, Florida, in March 1904, he suffered a stroke. Four months later, on July 8, he died from a second attack.[49] Obituaries appeared in major newspapers throughout the South. All the stores in Albany closed during the hours of his funeral as a sign of mournful respect and tribute for the passing of, the *Atlanta Constitution* wrote, "one of Albany's most prominent citizens."[50] The feelings of those who mourned his death were best expressed in a masonic tribute:

> He was truly a man among men, a giant in intellect, with a heart as tender as a woman's, and with an energy tireless and indomitable. Coming from a foreign land, he soon learned to admire and love American institutions, and became a patriot sincere and true. By sheer force of character and ability, he rose from humble beginnings to a position of power and dignity in the community. . . . He has left a legacy to his children, to his State and to Masonry — the legacy of an upright life, an untarnished name and a mind and heart imbued with high and lofty ideals.[51]

Similar statements of condolences poured in from all over the region. Eulogies and memorial resolutions were read in many B'nai B'rith and masonic lodges. The extent of his reknown was such that notices of his death appeared in publications as far away as Germany.[52]

Charles Wessolowsky, who has since his death slipped into historical oblivion, left little of material value behind. To his children, however, he left something perhaps that was of greater worth. His bequeathment was an optimistic and idealistic outlook on life that he converted into reality. "Uncle Charles never stopped saying," reflected Sadie Davis, "that if you are daring enough to touch life you will find that it is good, comforting and rewarding."[53]

On his tombstone, Charles Wessolowsky wanted inscribed his place of birth, the dates of his life and the statement "Past Grand High Priest of Georgia." He wanted to be remembered for that particular achievement because it, more than anything else, demonstrated the extent to which an immigrant Jew in America, with strength of character and force of drive, could enter into brotherhood with his Gentile neighbors while retaining both his identity as a Jew and a pride in his heritage.

FOOTNOTES

[1] The resolutions of expulsion were printed in the Thomasville *Weekly Times* no copies of which survive and were reprinted in the September 10th issue of the Macon *Journal & Messenger* and again in the September 12th issue of the Savannah *Daily Morning News*. For background on this incident, see Richard M. McMurry, "Rebels, Extortioners, and Counterfeiters: A Note on Confederate Judeaphobia," *Atlanta Historical Journal*, XXII (Fall-Winter 1978), 45-52; Louis Schmier, "Notes and Documents on the 1862 Expulsion of Jews From Thomasville, Ga.," *American Jewish Archives* XXXII (April 1980).
[2] Savannah *Daily Republican*, September 20, 1862.
[3] Telephone interview with Mrs. Sadie Gortatowsky Davis (Albany, Ga.), August 25, 1979.
[4] Savannah *Daily Republican*, September 20, 1862.
[5] Interview with Mrs. Sadie Davis, August 25, 1979.
[6] *Ibid.*
[7] Telephone interview with Mrs. Sadie Davis, May 30, 1979.
[8] Natchez *Daily Democrat*, June 1, 1878; Baton Rouge *Daily Advertiser*, May 26, 1878.
[9] Interview with Mrs. Sadie Davis, August 25, 1979.
[10] *Ibid.*
[11] *Records of R. G. Dun & Co., Georgia*, Vol. 35, p. 175, Harvard School of Business, Baker Library, Manuscript Division. Hereafter cited as *R. G. Dun & Co.*
[12] Chatham County, Georgia, Probate Court, *Record of Marriage Licenses, 1851-1866*, p. 101.
[13] *Population Schedules of the Eighth Census of the United States, 1860*, Microcopy No. T-635, roll 140.
[14] *R. G. Dun & Co, Georgia*, Vol. 35, p. 172.
[15] *The War of Rebellion Official Records of the Union and Confederate Armies*. Washington: Government Printing Office, Series I, *passim*.
[16] Charles Wessolowsky, *Compiled Service Records of Confederate Soldiers Who Served in Organizations from the State of Georgia*, National Archives, Microcopy No. 266.
[17] *R. G. Dun & Co., Georgia*, Vol. 35, p. 172.
[18] *Purse's Directory of the City of Savannah* (Savannah: Purse & Son, 1866), p. 142; National Archives, Record Group 58, Department of the Treasury, Records of the Internal Revenue Service, *International Revenue Assessment Lists*, 1865-1866, District 1, Division 8, annual 1866. Hereafter cited as *IRAL*.
[19] Savannah *Daily News & Herald*, July 7, 1866; *Ibid.*, August 28, 1866; Interview with Mrs. Sadie Davis, August 25, 1979; *IRAL*, District 1, Division 5, annual 1866.
[20] *R. G. Dun & Co., Georgia*, Vol. 10, p. 290.
[21] *Ibid.*, p. 291.
[22] *Ibid.*; interview with Mrs. Sadie Davis, August 25, 1979.
[23] *American Israelite*, August 20, 1869. Microfilm copies of the *Israelite* are to be found at the American Jewish Periodical Center at Hebrew Union College, Cincinnati, Ohio, as well as at HUC's Los Angeles campus.
[24] *The Jewish South*, November 15, 1879. Microfilm copies of this newspaper are located at the American Jewish Periodical Center at Hebrew Union College, Cincinnati, Ohio.
[25] *The Jewish South*, October 14, 1877; Albany *Herald*, July 8, 1904; Albany, Ga., Albany Hebrew Congregation, *Book of Sermons by Laymen and Members, 1870-1895*, American Jewish Archives, Box X-127.
[26] Lowndes County, Georgia, Court of Ordinary, *Marriage Book — White*, Vol. A, pp. 52, 257.
[27] *American Israelite*, August 20, 1869; *Ibid.*, October 21, 1870; interview with Mrs. Sadie Davis, May 30, 1979; Albany, Ga., Albany Hebrew Congregation, *Hebrew Ladies Benevolent Society Minute Books, 1876-1957*, entries of February 20, 1878 and February 17, 1901. American Jewish Archives, Box X-166; Albany, Ga., Hebrew Ladies Benevolent Society, *The Golden Jubilee and Memorial Fund*, p. 153. American Jewish Archives, Box X-129.
[28] Interview with Mrs. Sadie Davis, August 25, 1979.
[29] Letter to author from Carl F. Lester, Secretary of the Grand Lodge of Georgia, February 1, 1978.
[30] Albany *News*, December 21, 1869.

[31] *Ibid.*, December 28, 1869.
[32] Natchez *Daily Democrat*, June 1, 1878.
[33] *History and Reminiscences of Dougherty County, Georgia* (Albany, Ga.: n.p., 1924), pp. 82-95; *Manual and Biographical Register of the State of Georgia for 1871-2* (Atlanta: Plantation Publishers, 1872), p. 114; Albany *Herald*, July 8, 1904.
[34] *The Jewish South*, October 14, 1877.
[35] *History and Reminiscences of Dougherty County, Georgia*, pp. 95-102.
[36] *The Jewish South*, October 14, 1877.
[37] Savannah *Daily News & Herald*, July 7, 1866.
[38] *The Jewish South*, March 20, 1878.
[39] *Ibid.*, February 8, 1878.
[40] *Ibid.*, October 14, 1877.
[41] From the tone of the announcement of Wessolowsky's appointment it seems that Browne had to guarantee to him the right of free expression on any issue, *Ibid.*
[42] *Ibid.* Wessolowsky remained Associate Editor of *The Jewish South* even after it moved its offices to New Orleans in 1879. He was "replaced" by Rabbi Voorsaenger in August, 1881. *The Jewish South*, August 5, 1881, Manuscript Division, Tulane University.
[43] *Ibid.*, October 14, 1877-December 26, 1879. With the exception of the August 5, 1881 issue no copies of *The Jewish South* are known to exist for the years 1880-1882.
[44] *Ibid.*, July 19, 1878.
[45] *Ibid.*, July 12, 1878.
[46] Albany *Herald*, July 8, 1904.
[47] *History and Reminiscences of Dougherty County, Georgia*, pp. 200-207.
[48] Letter of Carl F. Lester, February 1, 1978.
[49] Albany *Herald*, July 8, 1904.
[50] Atlanta *Constitution*, July 9, 1904; Savannah *Daily Morning News*, July 9, 1904.
[51] *Excerpts From the Grand Lodge Proceedings for the Year, 1904* contained in a letter from J. E. Mosely, Worshipful Grandmaster of the Grand Lodge of Georgia, to the author, February 3, 1978.
[52] *Beilage zur Allgemeinen Zeitung des Judentums*, August 5, 1904, p. 5. American Jewish Periodical Center, Hebrew Union College, Cincinnati, Ohio.

Immigrant Jewish Women in Los Angeles: Occupation, Family and Culture*

Norma Fain Pratt

The Hamburger Home for Working Girls
Courtesy of Norma Fain Pratt

When Rachel Holtman, editor of the woman's page of the New York Yiddish newspaper *Freiheit,* visited Los Angeles in the 1930s she was surprised to discover a lively community of immigrant Eastern European Jewish women involved in local trade unions, in politics, and in Jewish cultural activities. She especially praised the program of the Los Angeles area's ten *lern kreyzn,* women's reading groups, in which the participants, mainly housewives and needle trades workers, were experiencing a complex process of self-education and social action. "These women," she enthusiastically noted in her autobiography, *Meyn lebns veg,* "take a fine fresh look at the world."

Beside this one rare comment about Jewish working women in Los Angeles in the 1930s, the rest has been silent; unfortunately, the sum and substance of the lives of the vital pioneer generation of Eastern European Jewish women in Los Angeles has remained unexplored by contemporary historians. Using communal records, oral history interviews, the Los Angeles Jewish press, a few autobiographies, some women's poetry, this article initiates an historical study into the structure of immigrant Jewish women's lives and into their roles and functions in Los Angeles society in the period between 1900 and 1940. Particularly, I will be examining the economic role of immigrant Jewish women, their participation in the transformation of Jewish culture and their efforts to develop new concepts of womanhood.

The Eastern European Jewish immigration to Los Angeles began in earnest almost a generation after the first wave of immigration from Europe to the Eastern part of the United States; that is, the Eastern European Jews settled in Los Angeles in significant numbers only after 1900. In 1900 the Jewish population of Los Angeles, mainly composed of German Jewish immigrants who had themselves arrived and prospered in Los Angeles in the mid-nineteenth century, was about 2,500. By 1907 the Eastern European immigration increased the population to about 14,000 and in 1920 there were over 20,000 Jews in Los Angeles. It is in the 1920s that the California boom took place and by the beginning of the Depression in 1929 the Jewish population had increased to 70,000. Thus, according to Max Vorspan and Lloyd P. Gartner, authors of a recent history of Los Angeles, "the Jews of Los Angeles, multiplying almost thirtyfold, more than kept pace with the fourfold increase in American Jewry. The rise in Jewish inhabitants exceeded even the boom rate of increase in the city."[2]

Why Eastern Europeans came to Los Angeles varied but the most frequent reasons given were poor health, then family reunion and then search for economic opportunity. Los Angeles' unpolluted air was commonly believed to be a healthgiving element contributing to the cure of tuberculosis. This health factor, therefore, was unique in the general motives which compelled Jewish migration in the United States. Interestingly, this health factor tended to emphasize the importance of the woman in the migrating family. For example, often enough it was the mother who made the family decision to move from New York, Baltimore or Chicago to Los Angeles when children became ill. Or a wife would assume special responsibility when her husband became ill, could not work and the family went with him to the land of oranges and palm trees; mothers worked in the period of father's convalescence.

This pattern was true in the case of several women I interviewed. For instance, Esther Aptheker migrated from Pinsk to New York in 1907. After marriage in 1913, she insisted that her husband, a presser in a cloakmakers' factory, move with her to Los Angeles in order to avoid catching tuberculosis in that "drafty New York City." She described her sense of relief to be living in Los Angeles which she called "*a gan eydn oyf der velt*," a heaven on earth.[3]

Another woman, Rachel Anna Kositza reminisced in her autobiography, *Zikhroynes fun a Bialystoker froy* (Memoirs of a woman from Bialystok), about the circumstances that brought her to Los Angeles. In this rare autobiography Kositza described how she emigrated to New York in 1906 after the infamous Bialystok pogrom. She and two children had been left behind by her husband in Europe. Instructed to wait until he called for her, she labored in a woolen factory and waited three years to no avail. Experiencing the terror of the pogrom, she decided to flee to America without her husband's permission. They were reunited in New York, settled down and had another child. Within a few years one of the children became tubercular. Borrowing money from relatives in New York, she left with the sick child to live with a brother (who also suffered from T.B.) and his wife in Los Angeles. Kositza found employment as a dress hemmer in a small dress factory on Spring Street and she lived in Boyle Heights, a district described in 1945 by sociologist Herbert Alexander as "the one community in Los Angeles to approximate the proletarian living standards of an urban Jewish community."[4] Kositza sent money home to her husband for the support of the two healthy children who had remained in his care. A year later she was able to send enough money for her husband, the children and her mother, a recent emigre, to travel to California.[5]

Most Eastern European Jewish women migrating to Los Angeles did not have to bear as great a financial burden alone as did Rachel Anna Kositza. Nevertheless, as historians have noted, in general Eastern European women traditionally played important economic roles in the family in Europe;[6] they continued this function in America and in Los Angeles.[7] In the City of Angels the occupations of Eastern European Jewish male immigrants did not differ greatly from the usual pursuits of Jewish immigrants back in the East. They were shopkeepers, needle trades workers, artisans, clerks; a few were peddlers and a few professionals. The Los Angeles immigrants, like their East coast brethren, also exhibited a pattern of so-called "upward mobility," moving into better businesses and into white collar work, at least by the 1930s.[8]

To what extent did female labor contribute to family subsistence, to "upward mobility," and at what cost to the female members of the family? Intriguing questions for which there are not conclusive answers as yet. But it can be said that the first generation of Eastern European women aided the family finances by providing housekeeping services to boarders and roomers, by performing home work, by running their own small shops or assisting in their husbands' stores and by working outside the home, particularly in the needle trade factories.[9] Women, of course, produced through reproduction. As Mitchell Gelfand, who is presently completing a Ph.D. thesis on the subject of the Los Angeles Jewish community, has suggested: "The large size of Jewish families also appeared to have aided the Jews, as it produced a reliable supply of family workers, at once more highly motivated and more willing to work for lower wages ...."[10]

In the period from 1920 through the early 1930s the most visible Jewish women in the Los Angeles labor force were garment workers, a few in women's wear but mainly working in men's clothing. Jewish women worked along with native American, Mexican and Italian women and men in several thousand small factories centered in the downtown area of the city.[11] In the 1920s Jewish women participated in the establishment and the administration of the Los Angeles trade union movement — first really organized in the early twenties, almost two decades after the International Ladies Garment Workers and the Amalgamated Clothing Workers were founded on the other side of the Mississippi. Organizing, running unions, and striking in Los Angeles was more difficult and more discouraging than in almost any city of the United States. As the International Ladies Garment Workers' Union trade organizer Rose Pesotta exclaimed in her autobiography *Bread Upon the Waters* on visiting Los Angeles in 1940: "Back in Southern California, land of sunshine and starvation wages, stronghold of the open shop."[12]

Most Jewish working class parents, in whatever city, did not want their daughters to become garment workers; this was particularly true in Los Angeles. For instance, by the 1930s, whenever possible Los Angeles girls received grammar school and high school educations equally along with their brothers although college remained mainly for males except among the most affluent.[13] Furthermore, it is quite interesting that the desire to keep young girls out of the "shops" virtually became part of the Jewish communal policy. That is to say, some of the Jewish community leaders, primarily wealthy German Jews, wanted Eastern European Jewish working girls to find sales and office jobs and wanted them to learn the amenities of middle class life. Deproletarianization, at least of the garment worker variety, was part of the Americanization process which German Jews had in store for their Eastern European brethren of the female gender. The following instance of the Hamburger Home reveals something of the occupational and cultural aspirations that some wealthy communal leaders had for poor unmarried girls.[14]

On February 10, 1928, through the special endowment of the Hamburger family a Home for Working Girls opened its portals to immigrant Eastern European unmarried women between the ages of 15 and 30 who had recently arrived in the city. Oddly enough, the wealth of the Hamburger family was established in 1881 when they opened the People's Store in downtown Los Angeles, "appealing to a working clientele for its cheaper line in merchandize."[15] The People's Store became the center of anti-trade union activity and David A. Hamburger was an organizer of the Employers' Association, formed to keep Los Angeles an open shop city.[16] The Hamburger Home for Working Girls was designed to discourage working girls from accepting a working class way of life. It was meant to give them a taste of opulence. Planning the building in 1927 Ida J. Wolfe, later the Head Resident, described how the "... facilities will enable most of the girls to have single rooms. We will have large living rooms, beaux parlors (which we feel to be a very necessary part of the young woman's life); a model kitchenette and a private dining room. This will make possible instruction in domestic science...."[17] Eventually the Home had its own Employment Committee. In an article in the Los Angeles *B'nai Brith Messenger*, "Home Surrounding for Jewish Working Girls," Wolfe explained its vocational goals:

> A girl often comes to us a total stranger, unfamiliar with the city and ignorant of its employment facilities or opportunities. For such a girl the Committee is a Godsend. After ascertaining her experience and qualifications, every effort is at once put forth in finding the right job for her. Constant contact is made and kept with the business houses and firms in the city. Many vocational adjustments between worker and employer have been accomplished through the interest of the committee members. The attempt of fitting the girl to the job and of training her for a better position has been worked out with a gratifying degree of success, and has opened a field of unlimited possibilities in the line of vocational guidance and training.[18]

Obviously, the girls were not to become garment workers but secretaries and salesladies and under the direct supervision of anti-union employers.

Parental aspirations and community programs succeeded in keeping the young Jewish female population of Los Angeles out of the shops. Studying the occupational statistics for Jewish women in Los Angeles in 1940, a significant increase in Jewish female white collar work is observable. One such report, the Kohs report published in 1942, compared the occupations of Jewish women and non-Jewish women (ethnic origins unfortunately were not specified) in Los Angeles in 1940. The statistics showed there were a substantially larger number of non-Jewish women engaged in professional fields of work (doctors, lawyers, school administrators, teachers) than Jewish women. However, the Jewish women workers were employed in the clerical and sales fields by an approximately seventy five percent greater ratio than non-Jewish workers. The report also stated that about twelve percent of Jewish women worked in manual trades and only 1 percent in domestic work in comparison with fifteen percent of non-Jewish women in manual trades and 12 percent non-Jewish women in domestic services.[19] Thus it appears that the major portion of the Jewish female wage earning work force in 1940 was composed of clerical workers. Both occupations requiring a great deal of education of work demanding very little formal schooling did not attract as much Jewish female participation.

Although several skilled and talented Eastern European Jewish women like the actress Vera Gordon or the Hollywood dress designer Clara Weiner achieved personal acclaim in an exceptional profession, the vast majority of educated Jewish women in Los Angeles, especially the university educated, worked as volunteers with the growing Jewish community network of cultural and social work organizations.[20] Like in other cities, the wealthier and older German Jewish residents were the first to develop a modern bureaucratic social work system to help the arriving immigrants as they first trickled into the city in the first decade of the twentieth century. This trickle turned into a torrent in the 1920s when the Jewish population of Los Angeles more than doubled. By the early 1920s a sophisticated welfare and adjustment system to process the various needs of the individual immigrant, the family, as well as to assuage the fear that the incoming Jews would provoke adverse criticism from non-Jewish neighbors was well underway. Significantly, most of the work with immigrants was performed by educated Jewish women of German background on a volunteer basis. In fact, by the early 1920s Jewish community social work was predominately a female occupation.

Most of the time social work required that women guide women because Jewish social work agencies in Los Angeles tended to focus the problems of family adjustment upon female adjustment. Their major preoccupations included household hygiene, the prevention of female juvenile delinquency, unmarried pregnancies and the education of children.[21] For example, the National Council of Jewish Women, an organization led by and composed of primarily Reform Jewish Women, accepted the greatest responsibility for teaching Eastern European women the ropes of life in America, or as they called it in those days, Americanization. In an article in the Los Angeles *California Jewish Review* on November 9, 1923 one Councilwoman offered insights into the activities and feelings of NCJW relative to their work with Eastern European immigrant women. "Gone are the days when women were content to be social butterflies," she explained. "Gone are the days when the few women who preferred 'higher studies' indulged in 'Browning Clubs;' ... when women went about as 'Lady Bountiful' with their sickening sentiments about charity work." The Councilwoman described the foundation of the Los Angeles Council's Immigrant Aid and Americanization Department in 1919 by Miss Jeanette Wrottenberg. "Most of the field workers who have been assisting Miss Wrottenberg," she noted "are university women, and it is through their sympathy and understanding that our American customs are translated and interpreted to the bewildered ones." Each field worker adopted a family and tried to adjust misunderstandings between the child "who quickly assimilates the American manner so strange to the slower mind of the adult and parents." The immigrant women were offered two kinds of education — either at home with a special home teacher or in a day school class under the auspices of the Los Angeles Board of Education. The Councilwoman was proud of the results of the women's educational program during its first four years — delighted with the Jewish women as students and as mothers:

> The Board of Education of Los Angeles reports show that 4,000 illiterate women have attended the classes in Americanization and a very high percentage of this number is Jewish ... one woman has already been prepared for High School and one has entered the university. It is no uncommon sight to behold these faithful students, plugging away at their lessons; students whose heads have been gently sprinkled with the silver of maturity ... for their ambition is to write a letter and read a newspaper so that they can be companions to their Americanized children.[22]

We can see that Americanization for immigrant Jewish women was clearly linked to their roles as mothers within the family.

Americanization for most Eastern European Jewish women also meant discarding some of the ancient orthodox rituals which had defined their womanhood: the mikvah (ritual bath), the baking of chalah, preparing of kosher food, the intoning of special female prayers in Yiddish from the *Tsena Urena*. In general, Jewish women had traditionally been the guardians of household religious practices. As they became more culturally American, they abandoned the symbols and the household practices of Jewish womanhood. It therefore became a subtle problem for Jewish women to remain Jews. In the period between 1900 and 1940 Orthodox Judaism lost a majority of its supporters among Eastern European Jews; these men and women were not attracted to Reform Judaism and they had only begun to create a new variety of American Judaism called Conservative Judaism. If anything, the transition from orthodoxy to culturally American modernity took place, for women, within the context of women's organizations. By the 1920s Jewish women's clubs including Hadassah, Young Women's Hebrew Association, Pioneer Women, Jewish Mothers Alliance of the United States, United Order of True Sisters, the Los Angeles Service League, Sigma Phi Sorority, Maccabean Zion Club, to name just a few groups which organized English speaking first and second generation Jewish women of Eastern European background, bloomed in the Los Angeles desert.[23] For these women, an essential portion of their Jewish identity was translated into a social identity with other Jewish women.

The fact that Jewish women began to define themselves in social terms rather than in family terms caused considerable anxiety among some Los Angeles community leaders in the 1920s. The changes which were taking place in education for women, in changing occupations, in social and religious practices had not yet been consciously understood. The changes were perceived as a threat to the traditional family and women were exhorted to remain within their former boundaries. For instance, as Rabbi Mayer Winkler of Reform Sinai Temple told his congregation one Friday night in November 1923 in a sermon entitled "The Ancient Jewess and Modern Ones":

> The life of the first mother Sarah serves as a model to the modern Jewess, too. According to the Midrash a dense cloud was hovering upon Sarah's tent during her lifetime. It protected her against dangerous influences from outside. Sarah, the prototype of real womanhood, wifehood, and motherhood, centered her actions about her home and in her home. The home of Sarah was a sanctuary in which the spirit of love, of harmony and of peace dwelt.[24]

Women also cautioned women against too much modernity. For example, one year after Rabbi Winkler's sermon an article appeared in the Yiddish language Los Angeles *California yidisher shtime,* written under the pseydonym "shayne Rokhl" (pretty Rachel) and entitled *"Yiden un di gantzkayt fun der mishpokhe,"* (Jews and family solidarity) in which the author claimed that anti-semites accuse Jews of teaching the pernicious doctrine of woman's independence and the necessary destruction of the patriarchical family. "Shayne Rokhl" declared this *bilbul* [libel] an out and out lie — perhaps true of a few Jewish Greenwich Village radicals in New York City but not true of the Los Angeles *kehillah.*[25]

"Shayne Rokhl" was not entirely correct. A radical Eastern European Jewish *intelligentsia* did reside in Los Angeles and to some extent these Jewish radicals had explored problems related to what they called the "woman's question"; some radicals even had experimented, in communes or in marriages without benefit of clergy, with new concepts of family life.[26] But the Los Angeles Jewish radicals did not devote much attention to the issues of personal individual change. They were mainly trade unionists, socialists, zionist-socialists or communists who energentically founded branches of the Workmen Circle, locals of the ILGWU and the ACW, political-literary magazines like *Zunland* and *Pasifik,* a sanitorium (to become the City of Hope), music societies and study groups.[27] The Los Angeles Jewish *radicaln* shared many of the characteristics of the Jewish Left in the East. It was a subculture, male and female, composed mainly of garment workers, small businesspeople, clerks, students, teachers, writers and artists who rejected religious Judaism but instead accepted a cultural Jewishness which they termed *Yiddishkayt.* This *Yiddishkayt* committed them to the preservation of spoken and written Yiddish; to the celebration of Jewish holidays; to the cultivation of Jewish loyalties, and to the support of the *arbeter classn* [working classes]. Their ideologies, often at war with each other, shared a belief in the possible creation of a distinct Jewish society as part of a culturally pluralistic society in America. They wanted to be nationally American (without assimilating); they wanted to express political radical ideals, especially about matters of social and economic injustices; they wished to remain linguistically Yiddish speakers and culturally Jews.[28]

In theory, the Jewish radicals believed in women's freedom and women's rights. And, in fact, women participated in the political organizations, in the trade unions, in the educational and social societies in a considerably more integrated way than their Orthodox, Reform or Conservative sisters. Nevertheless, women were not considered equal comrades and the division of the sexes in public life and in the private family domain was a pervasive reality. Some radical women dreamt of a new kind of equality with men. For example, Shifra Viess, a poet with no formal education, had joined the illegal socialist Jewish Labor Bund in Russia in 1905. She barely escaped police arrest by emigrating to the United States. Living first in Pittsburgh, then Chicago, she finally settled in Hollywood, California in 1917. Her poem, *"Mir, froyen,"* published in 1928 expressed the aspirations of married radicals of her generation:[29]

We rebuild the house and let in the sun: Husband, you are our brother Husband, you are our son.	Mir boyn-iber di shtiber un lozn areyn di zun; bistu man, unz a brider bistu man, unz a zun.
Equal captains with companion-husband and brother we help sail the ship to eternally new lands Hand and hand we both turn the steering wheel.	Gleykhe kapitanen, mit khaver-man un brider mir helfn firn di shifn tsu eybik neye lender hant-in-hant bym ruder.

* * *

In his massive study *World Of Our Fathers,* Irving Howe touched briefly upon the world of our mothers, that is upon the issue of the transformation of identity experienced by the Eastern European Jewish women in immigrant America. Rather too simply, he contended that women lost their importance in the family economy and remained essentially locked into marriage, motherhood and ladylike passivity. "Most Jewish girls," he noted in a summarizing statement "were neither wholly submissive nor wholly rebellious; within the bounds of the feminine role they found stratagems for cultivating the private interests and developing their private sensibilities." Only a very few, like Anzia Yezierska or Elizabeth Stern, both English-language wrtiers, tried to find a Woolfian "room with a view" but failed and ultimately "In some groping, half acknowledged way ... returned to the world of her fathers — a final reconciliation, of sorts."[30]

In my view the reality of the Eastern European Jewish female experience was considerably more complex. Drawing upon what happened between 1900 and 1940 in Los Angeles, it is possible to say, first, that the important economic role played by women in the family continued in America as did the family expectation that women would perform in the economic sphere. Of equal significance was the fact that Jewish women were not excluded from the ideals of "upward mobility"; they, like men, were expected to move out of the working class into the middle class on the basis of their own occupations through education. Moreover, these middle class ideals for women were present both within the family and were strongly reinforced by the organized Jewish community. In Los Angeles these factors resulted in a dramatic shift of the Jewish female working population from manual labor into clerical work by 1940.

Family remained the central focus for immigrant Jewish women and their daughters in the period between 1900 and 1940. The roles of wife and mother in Los Angeles were particularly emphasized by the problems of health care. In addition, Americanization and the burdens of adjustment in the new world through self education and children's education were placed squarely on the shoulders of women. In the process of discarding the old Eastern European ways, Jewish women within the family and within new social institutions became the culture bearers of a new American Jewish way of life; they did not, as Howe would have us believe, grope to return to the world of their fathers.

It is also possible to identify the seeds of a new definition of Jewish womanhood in the behavior of not just a few but of many women — especially from the 1920s onward. Definitions which transcended the narrow search of one's own little room with a view. Jewish women began to formulate definitions of female self which, while not denying the mother-wife roles, encompassed characteristics of independence and self expression along with an active concern for the public life of the Jewish community in America. Long before Eastern European men and their sons could acknowledge such concepts, women either were imagining or experimenting with a life balanced between family, self and the world. The new formulation did not reach fruition in the generation before 1940. It has remained an ideal for the generations yet to come.

FOOTNOTES

*This Paper was delivered at the session "The World Of Our Mothers, 1880-1940" at the Organization of American Historians Conference, San Francisco, April 10, 1980.

[1] Rachel Holtman, *Mayn Lebns veg (My Way in Life)* (New York, 1948), pp. 152-153. More information on radical women's *lern kreyzn* in Los Angeles is to be found in Minnie Yasshon, "Di lern-kreyzn bym YKUF in Los Angeles," ("Reading Groups of the YKUF in Los Angeles"), *Californier shriftn* (Los Angeles, 1961), pp. 84-86 and ibid. (Los Angeles, 1955), p. 230.

[2] Max Vorspan and Lloyd P. Gartner discuss the Los Angeles Eastern European Jewish migration to Los Angeles in *The History of the Jews of Los Angeles* (Philadelphia, 1970), pp. 109-119.

[1] Oral history interview with Esther Aptheker in Los Angeles was held in May 1978 by this author. The author also interviewed the following people in May and June 1978: Sara Lehrman, Anna Frazier and Sophie Silver (needle trades unions); Isaac Ronch (Yiddish journalist); Abraham Kindzer (labor editor of the communist Yiddish *Freiheit* in Los Angeles); Brokhe Kudly (Yiddish poet). The author used the tapes of the Los Angeles Federation Jewish Family Services Oral History Project. The interviews consulted were with Eleanor Siegman, Clara Weiner, Paula Williams, Selma Benjamin, Anna Block, Annie Lampl and Clara Kessler. The author also consulted the tape of an interview with the Jewish anarchist Dora Keyser from the the Feminist History Research Project under the direction of Sherna Gluck, California State University, Long Beach.

[4] Herbert Alexander, *Survey of Jewish Population: Los Angeles 1945* (Los Angeles, 1945), p. 20.

[5] Rachel Anna Kositza, *Zikhroynes fun a Bialystoker froy (Memoirs of a Woman From Bialystok),* (Los Angeles, California, 1964), pp. 119-128.

[6] For a discussion of the economic role of Eastern European Jewish women in Europe see Charlotte Baum, "What Made Yetta Work? The Economic Role of Eastern European Jewish Women in the Family," *Response*, No. 18 (Summer 1973).

[7] See Charlotte Baum, Paula Hyman and Sonya Michel, *The Jewish Woman in America* (New York 1976).

[8] The economic structure of Eastern European Los Angeles Jewry is discussed in Vorspan and Gartner, *History of the Jews of Los Angeles*, pp. 120-134. Mitchell Gelfand describes Jewish upward mobility in his article "Progress and Prosperity: Jewish Social Mobility in Los Angeles in the Booming Eighties," *American Jewish History*, LXVIII, 4 (June 1979), 408-433.

[9] In recent years there has been a growing historical literature dealing with theoretical issues in relation to women, work and the family. See the following for an introductory bibliography: Louise A. Tilly and Joan W. Scott, *Women, Work, and Family* (New York, 1978); Patricia Hilden, "Family History vs. Women in History: A Critique of Tilly and Scott," *International Labor and Working Class History*, No. 16 (Fall 1979), 1-11; Maurine Weiner Greenwald, "Historians and the Working-class Woman in America," ibid., No. 14/15 (Spring 1979), 23-32; Milton Cantor and Bruce Laurie, (eds.), *Class, Sex and the Woman Worker* (Westport, Conn., 1977); Thomas Kessner and Betty Boyd Caroli, "New Immigrant Women at Work: Italians and Jews in New York City, 1880-1905,"*Journal of Ethnic Studies*, V, 4 (Winter 1978), 19-31.

[10] Mitchell Gelfand, "Demographic and Quantitative Sources For The Study of Women in America," unpublished paper delivered at the Pacific Coast Women's Studies Conference, Univerity of Southern California, May 1978.

[11] Vorspan and Gartner, *History of the Jews of Los Angeles*, pp. 120-134.

[12] Rose Pesotta, *Bread Upon the Waters* (New York, 1944), p. 332. For a general history of the labor movement in Los Angeles see Louis B. Perry and Richard Perry, *A History of the Los Angeles Labor Movement, 1911-1941* (Berkeley and Los Angeles, 1963) and Grace Heilman Stimson, *Rise of the Labor Movement in Los Angeles* (Berkely and Los Angeles, 1955). For information on the labor movement and Jews in Los Angeles see, for example, the International Ladies Garment Workers' Union official publication *Justice* (New York), November 26, 1920; May 13, 1921; July 29, 1922; October 7, 1927; Febtuary 17, 1928; November 30, 1928; June 7, 1929; May 1, 1930 and May 16, 1930.

[13] According to Mitchell Gelfand's statistical analysis of the 1900 Federal Census for Los Angeles (Ph.D. dissertation, Carnegie Mellon University, in progress), as early as 1900 Jewish girls were receiving about the same number of elementary and secondary school years of attendance as Jewish boys. That this pattern continued has been corroborated substantially by several of my oral history interviews.

[14] The Hamburger Home presently is being used as a home for emotionally disturbed young women. The Home has a small archive of scrapbooks, mainly containing clippings, which date from the 1920s to the present.

[15] Vorspan and Gartner, *History of the Jews of Los Angeles*, p. 121.

[16] Ibid.

[17] "Jewish Alliance Center Work — Educational and Recreational," Los Angeles *B'nai Brith Messenger*, March 4, 1927. Clipping in the Scrapbook Collection of the Hamburger Home, Los Angeles.

[18] Ida J. Wolfe, "Home Surroundings for Jewish Working Girls," *ibid.*, December 14, 1928. Clipping in the Scrapbook Collection of the Hamburger Home.

[19] Samuel C. Kohs with Louis H. Blumenthal, "Survey of the Recreational and Cultural Needs of the Jewish Community of Los Angeles Conducted by the National Jewish Welfare Board, 1942," typescript copy in the private library of Fred Maserik, Professor of Industrial Relations,

University of California, Los Angeles, 19 parts, separately paged (hereafter cited as Kohs Survey), Part, "Vocational and Educational Guidance together with an analysis of the Occupational Distribution of the Jews in Los Angeles," pp. 25-42. For studies that compare the occupation distribution of Jewish women with other ethnic women workers see Kessner and Caroli,. "New Immigrant Women at Work: Italians and Jews in New York City, 1880-1905" and Corinne Azen Krause, "Grandmothers, Mothers and Daughters: An Oral History Study of Ethnicity, Mental Health, and Continuity of Three Generations of Jewish, Italian, and Slavic-American Women," typescript publication of the Institute on Pluralism and Group Identity of the American Jewish Committee, n.d., consulted at the American Jewish Archives, Hebrew Union College, Cincinnati.

[20] For biographical information about Vera Gordon see, *Who's Who in American Jewry*, 1926 (New York, 1926), p. 226; *Zunland: California Jewish Diamond Jubilee* (Los Angeles, 1925), pp. 45-48 and Joseph L. Malamut, ed., *Southwest Jewry*, 3 vols (Los Angeles, 1926, 1927 and 1955), I, p. 76. Biographical information on several volunteer Jewish women community leaders are to be found in *Who's Who in American Jewry* (New York, 1926, 1927, 1938) and in *Southwest Jewry* (Los Angeles, 1926, 1927 and 1955).

[21] For records of social work activities with family, children and women see the Los Angeles National Council of Jewish Women Papers including the Book on Executive Meetings and Funds 1911-1915; Minutes of the Chidren's Bureau 1924-1931 and Bulletin of the National Council of Jewish Women (Los Angeles Section), April-November 1937. There is extensive material about Jewish juvenile delinquency in Los Angeles in the Kohs Survey, "Report on Juvenile Delinquency." For example, statistics prepared for Kohs by Dora Berres, Executive Director of the Children's Bureau of the National Council of Jewish Women for the period 1930-1941 state "Number of Jewish maladjusted, neglect, abused girls, or girls with special problems, under the care of the Council Children's Bureau . . . are as follows:

1941 — 451 (for 11 months)   1936 — 661
1940 — 607   1934 — 697
1939 — 619   1932 — 873
1938 — 672   1930 — 335

(Kohs Survey, "Report on Juvenile Delinquency, p. 67).

[22] Los Angeles Section Council of Jewish Women," Los Angeles *California Jewish Review*, November 9, 1923.

[23] By 1942 there were forty-two women's organizations belonging to the Los Angeles Conference of Jewish Women's Organizations. For the list see Kohs Survey, "Jewish Congregations, Secular Organizations and Citizenship Activities for Jews," p. 20 and *ibid.*, submitted by Louis B. Blumenthal, "Report on the Jewish Community Center of the Jewish Centers Association of Los Angeles," p. 84. These lists do not include women's organizations belonging to the socialist and communist Jewish Left.

[24] Excerpt from a sermon given by Rabbi Mayer Winkler at the Los Angeles Sinai Temple reprinted in the Los Angeles *California Jewish Review*, November 9, 1923.

[25] "Shayne Rokhl," *"Yidn un di gantzkayt fun der mishpokhe,"* (Jews and Family Solidarity), Los Angeles *California ydisher shtime*, July 18, 1924.

[26] For example, see the biographic statement about the life of the Yiddish poet Aida Glazer in E. Korman, *Yidishe dikhterin (Yiddish Women Poets)* (Detroit, 1928), pp. 340-341.

[27] An institutional description of the Los Angeles Jewish political left can be found in "notizen," (Notes), Los Angeles *Pasifik*, I (March 1929), 45-50.

[28] A recent study of Jewish radicalism in America is Arthur Liebman, *Jews and the Left* (New York, 1979).

[29] Shifra Viess, *"mir, froyen"* ("We, women"), New York *Der hamer* (September 1928), p. 50. The English translation is the author's. For biographical information about Viess see Zalman Reisen, *Leksikon fun der yidisher literatur, prese un filologie*, 2 vols (Vilna, 1928), p. 261 and *Leksikon fun der nayer yidisher literatur*, 7 vols (New York, 1956), III, p. 400.

[30] Irving Howe, *World Of Our Fathers: The Journey Of The East European Jews to America And The Life They Found And Made* (New York and London, 1976), pp. 265-271.

Francis E. Abbot: Perceptions of a Nineteenth Century Religious Radical on Jews and Judaism*

Benny Kraut

Francis E. Abbot
(1836-1903)
Courtesy of the
Harvard University Archives

Introduction: The last third of the nineteenth century witnessed a dramatic upsurge of religious liberalism, radicalism, and freethought in the United States. In the midst of these religious developments, some liberal Jewish and Christian intellectuals and theologians took increasing cognizance of each other's thinking and activities. While a minor movement in terms of numbers and restricted generally to clergy, scholars of religion, and the more educated laymen, this intellectual rapprochement nevertheless represented a significant new chapter in American Jewish-Christian relations.

In an era when many liberal Jewish and Christian thinkers professed belief in a "religion of humanity," a universal religion which would unite mankind, it was perhaps historically inevitable that some would seek to familiarize themselves with each other's religious traditions and band together to acknowledge mutual religious interests.[1] Not a few had realized that the affirmation of religious liberalism or radicalism logically necessitated associating with people of differing religious points of view. Thus, some very eminent Jewish and Christian liberals joined the Boston-based Free Religious Association (F.R.A. — founded in 1867) which dedicated itself to the creation of a free and open platform for intellectual religious discourse, to the promotion of religious liberty and the uprooting of religious authoritarianism, and to the scientific study of religion. Open to members of all faiths and no faiths, the F.R.A. represented the first organized American association featuring Christians and Jews discussing religion and theology from the same lecture platform, and therefore, in a sense, could be regarded as the first Jewish-Christian interfaith organization in America.[2] Then too, Christian and Jewish thinkers at this time also read each other's liberal press (Jews read *The Index*; Christians read *The Israelite* and *The Jewish Times*), and some Jewish and Christian liberal clergy exchanged pulpits.[3] To a limited extent, moreover, laymen participated in or even joined radical religious societies springing up outside their own religious tradition; Felix Adler's New York Society for Ethical Culture attracted individuals of Christian origin, while O.B. Frothingham's Independent Liberal Church in New York and other such groups attracted some Jews.

But how deeply did this religious and intellectual rapprochement between liberal Jews and non-Jews really extend, and did it manifest itself in some form of social interaction? What were the limits of its theological accommodation? How were Jews and Judaism actually perceived? By analyzing the attitude and relationship to Jews and Judaism of Francis Ellingwood Abbot (1836-1903), one of the foremost and incisive religious radicals of his day, some rather suggestive answers to these questions will be forthcoming. While Abbot's religious ideology was far more radical than most, his views on Jews and Judaism nevertheless broadly reflected both mainstream Christian religious liberalism and religious free-thought.[4]

Born in Boston on November 6, 1836 into an old and distinguished Puritan family, Francis Ellingwood Abbot was a brilliant, passionate man who ultimately became a storm-center of the American religious freethought movement in the post-Civil War period.[5] Typical of many of New England's finest minds, Abbot was channeled into a career as a Unitarian minister. He was graduated from Harvard College in 1854, ordained in 1863 by the Meadville Theological School in Meadville, Pa., and became pastor of the Unitarian Church in Dover, N.H., in June 1864.

Like a number of his social and religious peers, however, Abbot's religious thinking took an increasingly radical turn during the 1860's. He was greatly influenced by the modern currents of European scholarship — Bible Criticism, comparative religion, Darwinism and the ideas of progress and evolution, self-sufficiency of reason and the scientific method — all of which were making inroads into American religious, cultural, and intellectual life. Abbot came to repudiate all religious dogmas and creeds and to staunchly oppose any form of religious authority placing constraints on free religious expression and hindering the pursuit of knowledge on a sound scientific basis.

Unhappily for Abbot, his personal religious development came at a time when the Unitarian movement, seeking denominational unity and a centrist theological consensus, adopted a Unitarian Constitution at the National Conference of Unitarian Churches, April 4-6, 1865, whose preamble formally subscribed to the "Lordship of Jesus Christ."[6] Abbot, along with a few other Unitarian radicals such as Octavius B. Frothingham, William T. Potter and Edward C. Towne, interpreted Unitarianism in the most universal religious terms and objected to this language as both a betrayal of individual religious liberty and an expression of unacceptable sectarianism. One year later, at the First Annual Meeting of the National Conference of Unitarian Churches at Syracuse, October 10-11, 1866, Abbot moved to have the objectionable language replaced with a substitute preamble of his own. After heated debate, his motion was decisively defeated by majority vote. Abbot then perceived himself to stand outside not only of Unitarianism, but of the Christian consensus generally. From the late 1860's on, he became a self-avowed anti-Christian and one of the most trenchant religious-intellectual polemicists against Christianity on the American scene.

Abbot responded to his new religious situation by energetically thrusting himself into the myriad liberal religious, social, and political causes of the day. Together with Potter and Frothingham, he was instrumental in founding the Free Religious Association in 1867, and he became its most systematic and religiously radical thinker. He also played a role in the free-church movement, accepting the position of minister to the Independent Church in Toledo, Ohio (1869-1873) only after it had dropped its Unitarian name and affiliation.[7] From Jaunary 1, 1870 until June 1, 1880, with only occasional breaks, Abbot edited *The Index (A Weekly Paper Devoted to Free Religion)* and turned it into one of the most distinguished and influential papers of the liberal and free religious movement. An impassioned and zealous advocate of the separation of church and state doctrine, Abbot spearheaded a petition drive to Congress in 1872 against a proposed "Christian Amendment" to the Constitution, and organized the National Liberal League in 1876 to actively promote the complete separation of church and state.[8]

Through these activities in the late 1860's and 1870's Abbot had the opportunity to become acquainted with with some of the leading Jewish Reform rabbis and Jewish laymen of his time, and from them he gained first-hand knowledge about modern Jews and Judaism.[9] At its annual Boston convention and at intermittent conventions sponsored by the F.R.A., he heard addresses (and/or later read them in the published *Proceedings* and other F.R.A. publications series) on the meaning of Reform Judaism and on the role of the Jews and Judaism in the future by Isaac M. Wise, Moritz Ellinger, S.H. Sonneschein, Max Lilienthal, and Raphael Lasker.[10] Some of these individuals, as well as others, became strong supporters of his National Liberal League.

Abbot took a clear interest in Jews and Judaism. He kept abreast of developments in Judaism and the Jewish community at home and abroad by reading the Anglo-Jewish press as well as news on Jewish affairs in the secular and Christian press. He enjoyed a newspaper subscription exchange with Wise's *Israelite* and Ellinger's *Jewish Times,* and seems also to have read from time to time the *Jewish Advance, Jewish Messenger,* and *Jewish Record.* Periodically, he published news about the Jewish community which he had gleaned as well as sermons and lectures by Jews in his *Index.*[11] No doubt Abbot also read some of the Jewish writings on Christianity, notably Isaac M. Wise's *The Origins of Christianity,* (1868) which the author had expressly dedicated to the F.R.A.[12]

Abbot on Judiasm

Given his various contacts with and interest in Jews and Judaism, how did Abbot regard Judaism? To answer this question one must first distinguish between Abbot's perceptions of 'old' Biblical Judaism and the modern Reform variety.

Without question, Abbot's initial understanding of Judaism and its role in human civilization emerged from his readings of the Hebrew Bible and the New Testament and the religious interpretation of these literatures taught him by his parents and by instructors at Harvard and Meadville. From earliest times, Abbot was inculcated with the basic theological affirmation of Christianity with respect to Judaism, and retained it throughout his life: Christianity superseded Judaism and Jesus was Judaism's most perfect flower. Important to note is that Abbot's assimilation of modern critical studies in Bible and religion did not at all alter this basic conviction. The writings of Strauss, Bauer, Martineau, Renan, among others — regardless of their evaluation of Christianity — all took for granted the superiority of Christianity over Biblical and post-Biblical Judaism, and that Christianity embodied the natural fulfillment and universal expression of a narrow, tribal Judaism. Most every nineteenth century Christian — conservative, liberal or radical, Scriptural literalist or critic — affirmed that same basic belief.[13]

It is not surprising, therefore, that Abbot proclaimed Jesus "as a preacher of purely spiritual truth" to stand "at the head of all the great religious teachers of the past,"[14] and that in Jesus' soul, "the great aspiration of the Hebrew race became purified from its alloys and stamped forever with the impress of his superior spirit."[15] Therefore, Abbot contended, "Christianity is the natural development of Judaism. Judaism is germinal Christianity; Christianity is fructified Judaism."[16] And while he lauded the prophets as significant reformers and highly progressive in their day, espousing as they did the ideas of monotheism, covenant, and reward and punishment, their nationalist orientations were, to Abbot, "in part, at least, ... crude and narrow." Moreover, his religious bias against Biblical Jewry, nurtured by the bias of Protestant Bible scholarship, was quite apparent from the descriptive language he used. Thus, the prophets exhorted the nation to righteousness and attempted "to deepen the moral consciousness of the people," Abbot wrote, but "it *could hardly be expected* that an ignorant and headstrong semitic tribe should comprehend fully, and carry out into consistent practice, the principles which gave it all its historic importance, and which marked out for it a magnificent destiny. Retrogression and unfaithfulness to the law of its own being was *sure to appear in the history of such a people.*"

Abbot's attitude to modern Reform Judaism, the preeminent form of American Judaism in the 1870's, was far less uniform. In fact, it furnishes a revealing account as to how Reform self-perceptions were received by a non-Jewish religious radical, because Abbot reacted to the two main thrusts of American Reform ideology from the 1860's on into the twentieth century: that Reform Judaism was free from dogma and creeds, and therefore fully in consonance with the modern liberal world; and, that rational Reform Judaism was the universal religion of the future for all mankind.[18]

In the 1870's Abbot sincerely welcomed the emergence and rise of Reform Judaism as a compelling, positive sign of the times. In Reform's streamlining of ritual forms, in its rejection of Jewish national identity, in its dismissal of supernatural beliefs such as a personal Messiah and bodily resurrection, in its allying itself to science, evolution, liberalism, and universalism, Abbot found a vindication of his understanding of historical religious progress and his religious teleology.

In accord with most religious and intellectual liberals and radicals, Abbot believed that all organized religions were but progressive phases in the evolution of religion, historically contingent products destined to disappear. With the beliefs, ritual forms, and institutions of all religions molded by specific historical circumstances which constantly change, all religions were historically limited and none could claim to be the absolutely spiritual universal religion of the future.[19] But Abbot sensed that a new religious age was dawning, and he heralded the imminent arrival of a truly universal religion transcending all organized religions. He identified this religion with "free religion," that is, a religion emancipated from "the outward law," voluntarily "obedient to the inward law," a religion whose "great faith or moving power is faith in man as a progressive being." Furthermore, he steadfastly believed that he could scientifically demonstrate that "Free Religion is the natural outcome of every historical religion — the final unity, ... towards which all historical religions slowly tend." In the growth of mankind into Free Religion "lies the only hope of the spiritual perfection of the individual and the spiritual unity of the race."[20]

Looking around him, Abbot discerned substantial processes of liberalization occurring "in several of the great historic religions," and he interpreted these trends as "marked signs of progressive movement on converging lines towards a common faith and fellowship."[21] The reforming of Judaism was an integral part of that trend, and Abbot applauded. Reform Judaism, by stripping away many observances and beliefs, was positive proof for Abbot that organized religions were dying and that Reform Jews and liberal Christians were gradually slipping out of their religious moorings and would soon unite in a transcendent fellowship of free religion.

Abbot's impressions of Reform Judaism and his anticipation of its gradual disappearnace were neither totally naive nor altogether ill-founded. The various speeches, sermons, and articles on Reform which he had heard or read reiterating the creedlessness of Reform Judaism and its commitment to religious universalism understandably led him to his conclusions. At the first annual meeting of the F.R.A., May 28-29, 1868 he heard Rev. I. S. Nathans of Boston inform those assembled that Reform Jews have "overcome Orthodox Jewish prejudices," no longer hope for a Messiah or the reestablishment of Jerusalem, and truly seek religious union with fellow religious liberals. Jews, liberal Unitarians, and rationalist thinkers should unite to disseminate rational religious truths throughout the world, Nathans argued. And he concluded: "Judaism has always been a true vindicator of pure, clear Unitarianism, and will, under a scientific rational reform, join to fulfill the closing of the prayer, 'On this day may the Lord be one, and his name ... be one'."[23]

During the next decade, Abbot heard similar thoughts and other related ideas from more prominent Jews. Moritz Ellinger, editor of the *Jewish Times* and one of the most radical of Reform Jews, proclaimed Reform Judaism to be unsectarian and reconcilable with all phases of modern thought, characterized the Bible as but the first rather than the last record of divine ideas among men, and denied that Judaism alone confers salvation.[24] At the annual F.R.A. convention nine years later, Ellinger predicted the emergence by the end of the century of a religion of humanity based on reason and common human feelings uniting Jews and Christians. He suggested that the F.R.A., by bringing individuals of different religions together, was greatly facilitating the fulfillment of this goal.²⁵ Rabbi Isaac M. Wise echoed these sentiments, and reiterated his belief that Judaism knows no symbols, mysteries or dogmas; that Judaism is compatible with freedom and an ally of science; and that it acknowledges the supremacy of reason, conscience and history over faith.²⁶ At the seventh annual convention of the F.R.A., Abbot heard Rabbi S. H. Sonneschein repudiate the veracity of many Biblical stories and even intimate that intermarriage is permissible.²⁷ Professing himself to be a loyal devotee of free religion, Sonneschein ended his address with a flourish: "I tell you that the Jewish Rabbi of the Reformed school may dare to be in the fullest sympathy even with the results of the researches of my friend Abbot, who is Anti-Christian, and Anti-Jewish and anti anything! We say, give us truth, and in the face of truth, we shall acknowledge it."²⁸

Exposed to these as well as other expressions of Reform Judaism's religious universalism and identification with modern rational trends,²⁹ and aware of the ever increasing numbers of pulpit exchanges between rabbis and ministers,³⁰ Abbot was quite optimistic in the 1870's about the ultimate realization of his universalist religious vision.

Extremely pleased with Reform Judaism's progressive liberalism and anti-sectarianism, Abbot, however, consistently criticized what he perceived to be Reform's universalist pretentiousness. By and large most Reform thinkers Abbot encountered tended to identify Reform Judaism specifically as the universal religion of the future. For them, this ideological correspondence helped to justify continued Jewish existence and to harmonize Reform with the liberal hope of religious universalism.³¹ Ellinger noted that the "true spirit of Judaism was the religion of the universe."³² Wise was even more explicit. At the Second Annual Meeting of the F.R.A. in 1869, he voiced his familiar triumphal refrain: the Decalogue contains the essential spirit and law of Judaism, and "neither Christianity nor the Islam nor philosophy has been able to add to the Decalogue one principle on which human happiness depends, either here or hereafter." Wise, therefore, affirmed: ". . . I am morally certain that this [Religion of the Decalogue, which is pure Judaism] is the religion of the coming generations."³³ Rabbi Raphael Lasker of Boston also limned the religion of the future at an F.R.A. national meeting, citing its lack of mysteries, fear of one God, and its Sabbath as a day of rest. Indeed, Lasker concluded: "What I have delineated before you as the future religion of mankind is nothing but Judaism, modern Judaism."³⁴

Abbot dismissed such notions out of hand. Both Christianity and Judaism, "notwithstanding the incalculable services they have done to man, are perishing systems.³⁵"

No organized, historically rooted religion could become the universal religion. Thus, for example, while praising Ellinger's *Jewish Times* for "emphasizing the universal truths of Judaism," he rejected the paper's identification of Judaism with the universal religion of humanity.

> We have but one criticism to make upon its general position — the same which we have made upon so-called "Liberal-Christianity," — namely, that the universal religion of humanity requires the abolition of all those destructive features which separate historic religions from each other. ... Will our Jewish brothers learn to forget their nationality in the consciousness of our common humanity, and abandon the myths of their historical religion? The religion of the future will not be historical, but spiritual; and the sacrifice will be necessary. Reformed Judaism, like Liberal Christianity, is only a stepping-stone to a larger and higher faith.[16]

A few years later, when Isaac M. Wise again pronounced a pure, rational Judaism to be the religion of the future, Abbot responded. According to Wise, Abbot noted, "Judaism in its pure and denationalized form, will and must become the religion of all free men." Abbot, however, reminded his readers that "the enthusiastic devotees of every other religious denomination are ready to make the same prophecy concerning their own faith; but it is not wise [pun intended?] at present, to say what the name and form of the future religion 'will and must be'."[37]

Abbot's dual attitude to Reform Judaism, endorsing it as a sign of the times but rejecting its universalist self-perceptions, is perhaps best reflected in his reaction to Wise's call for a Union of American Hebrew Congregations. "We heartily wish our Israelite friends success in their undertakings," he remarked, "but we hope they will not forget *the broader interests of truth* in their aim to establish and advance the welfare of Hebrew congregations."[38] Not surprisingly, by the late 1870's, Abbot found Felix Adler's New York Society for Ethical Culture to offer the model society by which Jews could transcend their Judaism and participate in "the broader interests of truth." In the wake of the Kaufmann Kohler-Felix Adler controversy,[39] Abbot queried, "why should Judaism not advance to the broader ground of *perfect liberty of thought* so ably advocated by ... Professor Adler? We look with more hope to such societies as Mr. Frothingham's and Professor Adler's than to all the churches and synagogues together."[40]

Abbot on the Jews

Notwithstanding his reservations about Reform Judaism, Abbot commended the character and integrity of the Jews and defended their social, political, and religious rights. His *Index* took great pains to praise Jewish accomplishments and to reveal them for all to see. In addition, through the publication of editorials, brief notices, letters to the editor, rabbinic essays, and foreign news dispatches, the *Index* reported on and objected to the discrete forms of Christian religious hostility and discrimination to which Jews were subject both in the United States and Europe.

Abbot's concern for the Jews was not motivated by any personal attachments or singular affection for Jews as a socio-religious group.

Rather, Jewish achievements, as well as the discrimination which they suffered, contributed significant intellectual weapons — additional cannon fodder, so to speak — to his uncompromising polemical battle against Christianity and the church. The Christian church for Abbot, despite its previous accomplishments, represented but an organized association of spiritual slavery and authoritarianism.[41] Defining the essence of Christianity to inhere in its belief in Jesus as the Messiah,[42] Abbot therefore argued that the Christian religion set limits on intellectual liberty and restricted freedom of religious expression. He regarded Christian self-affirmation of salvation only through Christ — a necessary Christian belief in his interpretation of Christianity — to result in an irrepressible conflict with the modern world, inevitably leading to intolerance, bigotry, and the political struggle in America to merge church and state.[43] By underscoring both Jewish virtue and Christian intolerance of the Jews, Abbot marshalled additional historical evidence to discredit what he considered to be the pernicious illiberality and clerical dogmatism of Christianity.[44]

Thus, Abbot sometimes explicitly contrasted positive Jewish qualities with negative Christian traits, such as Jewish rectitude and charity with Christian unprincipledness, prejudice and cruelty. The *Index*, for instance, reprinted a Sunday *Herald* account about a synagogue which refused to rent a pew to a convicted Jewish thief for fear that it would take tainted money. If Christian churches followed that rule, the *Herald* continued, they might "be exposed to bankruptcy."[45] On another occasion, Abbot cited the purchase of a small town by J. G. Bloch, a wealthy Warsaw Jewish banker, and commented: "... we have not heard that he refused to admit Christians to it any more than Mr. Judah Touro refused to admit Christians to Newport, R.I., when he owned the greater part of the town."[46] The innuendo is clear.

Sometimes Abbot's *Index* highlighted Jewish accomplishments achieved only in the face of Christian opposition. Hence, in listing the great contributions of Spinoza, the Rothschilds, Gambetta, Emilio Castelar, and Disraeli, the paper expressed joy that the Jews were at long last "able to pluck honors from Christendom's reluctant hand, and to bring themselves into the world's free parliament of thought and action."[47] Even Moslems treated Jews better than the Christians, the *Index* suggested, in its reprint of a European paper's report contrasting the favorable treatment of Jews by Moslem Turks with their outrageous persecution by Russian Christians.[48]

Within this context, it is reasonable to argue that even Abbot's recording of simple, forthright praise of the Jews, without explicit anti-Christian allusions, probably also held some polemical connotations. By complimenting Jews on the opening of a hospital for the sick irrespective of their creed,[49] by reprinting reports that Jews in Virginia were quite successful and that English Jews enjoyed prominent political positions,[50] by extolling Jews as excellent citizens,[51] and by reprinting a

Kaufmann Kohler essay on the Jews' contribution to civilization,[52] Abbot did not merely inform the public of Jewish progress and achievement, but also tacitly underlined the genuine folly of Christian bias and discrimination against the Jews.[53]

Specific acts against Jews evoked Abbot's contempt. He was disgusted with the social manifestations of Christian religious intolerance demonstrated in the Seligman-Hilton affair of 1877, and thought Wilhelm Marr's racial antisemitism ridiculous.[54] He mocked Christian missionary movements to the Jews, noting the vast discrepancy between the huge sums of money spent to convert Jews and the extraordinarily meagre results. He also ridiculed the occasional anti-Jewish outbursts of evangelists such as Dwight Moody and Ira Sankey.[55] On these issues, he let Jews speak for themselves in his *Index,* by publishing Rabbi Henry Gersoni's vitriolic letter denouncing Christian attempts to convert him,[56] and reprinting a *Jewish Times* article on a Jewish boy having been secretly converted to Christianity.[57] No editorial comment was necessary to inform the reader of Abbot's antipathy to such proceedings.

An ardent supporter of the principle of the separation of church and state, Abbot also devoted considerable space in his paper to the social and economic discrimination Jews experienced because of the incomplete fulfillment of that ideal. This focus was part of the more general, constant and spirited campaign he waged through the pages of the *Index* during the 1870's to have the doctrine of the separation of church and state fully implemented. Abbot's perceptions of Jewish disabilities were correct. Jews did suffer from the application of various Sunday Blue Laws and sectarian Bible readings in public schools, and they felt aggrieved by Thanksgiving Day Proclamations of government officials affirming the Christian nature of the country. Politically, they would have sustained an even greater setback had the United States Congress in 1874 approved the proposal of an evangelical and conservative Protestant coalition, the National Reform Association, to adopt a "Christian Amendment" to the Constitution formally and legally declaring the United States a Christian country[58]

American Jews protested vigorously on all these issues,[59] and Abbot used *The Index* to acknowledge their just claims. He reprinted Rabbi Max Lilienthal's essay on Cincinnati's nationally known public school issue concerning Bible readings in the classroom,[60] Rabbi Bernhard Felsenthal's public protest on Bible readings in Chicago's public school system,[61] and Rabbi Sabato Morais' objection to the use of a Christian text in the Philadelphia public school curriculum.[62] The *Index* also published the proceedings of an F.R.A. conference on the theme "Sunday Observance" at which Boston's Rabbi R. Lasker protested the fact that Jewish children must go to school on Saturday.[63] Abbot sometimes injected his own opinions on these issues as they affected Jews, agreeing with Isaac M. Wise that Supreme Court Justice Strong, a leading proponent of the "Christian Amendment" movement should be impeached,[64] and outlining the economic hardships Christian Sunday Laws imposed on Jews.

Publicizing these religiously motivated forms of prejudice which Jews experienced in the social and political arena was also part of Abbot's anti-Christian polemic. Abbot viewed these public discriminations as but a natural offshoot of Christian self-affirmation, and they confirmed his conviction that Christian influence in the public sector must be relentlessly fought and decisively defeated.

It is no wonder, then, that Abbot's multifarious organizational efforts through the 1870's to insure the separation of church and state won Jewish approval and support. His petition campaign in 1872 against the "Christian Amendment," resulting in over 30,000 signatures being sent to Congress and helping to defeat the drive in 1874, was both appreciated and congratulated in Jewish quarters.[66] His promotion of local Liberal Leagues, beginning in January 1873, to vigilantly guard against the encroachment of the church in state affairs and to demand the abolition of all special favors to the church also gained Jewish support, and some Jews joined local Leagues.[67] In 1876, at the Centennial Congress of Liberals held in Philadelphia July 1-4, Abbot successfully organized and became President of the National Liberal League which united local auxiliary Leagues into a national umbrella association.[68] Dedicated to the adoption of a "Religious Freedom Amendment" insuring the full separation of church and state, to the equitable taxation of all church property, to the total cessation of religious instruction and worship in public schools, and to the repeal of all laws enforcing the Sunday as the Sabbath,[69] the National Liberal League quickly gained the affiliation and loyalty of several influential Jewish clergy and laymen. Remarkably, but understandably, the issue of church-state relations precipitated a natural, pragmatic alliance uniting Jews, liberal Christians, religious freethinkers, and secularists in common bond, their religious and theological differences notwithstanding.

The depth of Jewish allegiance to Abbot's National Liberal League and its goals is clearly evident from the types of letters Abbot received from Jews responding to his request for their support. On May 10, 1876, Abbot wrote Rabbi Bernhard Felsenthal of Chicago asking that he join the League as a Vice-President. Felsenthal, a vociferous opponent of Bible readings in Chicago public schools, was "much flattered," and happily consented. "That I endorse heartily all the aims and objects of the League, I need hardly assure you," he replied. Indeed, he recommended to Abbot that Chicagoans Judge Booth, Henry Greenebaum, and E. Juessen should also be appointed to office because of their "sincere sympathy with all your endeavors" and their position of influence which "could do far more than I can for the furtherance of liberality in public life and national institutions."[70] Rabbis Isaac M. Wise and S. H. Sonneschein as well as Moritz Ellinger, all acquaintances of Abbot's from the F.R.A., were also asked to serve as Vice-Presidents. Only Sonneschein seems to have declined, though his reply has not been preserved. Wise pledged his support to Abbot. "I will work with you," he exclaimed, and he was "willing to be . . . officer or private, as it may be deemed most advantageous to the cause."[71] Ellinger replied "that I shall cheerfully contribute all that is in my power to the success of the cause in which I believe we labor in common."

Other rabbis joined the National Liberal League as well. Extant membership lists for 1876 include the names of Henry Gersoni of Atlanta, Max Schlesinger of Albany, and Max Landsberg of Rochester. Joseph Krauskopf of Cincinnati, though not yet ordained, is also listed. In expressing his support for the cause, Gersoni wrote Abbot that "curiosity as well as a desire to improve in wisdom by a personal acquaintance with the thinkers of your city, prompts me to visit that place where the star of liberalism rises so gloriously on a horizon of blue laws."[73] Schlesinger spoke at the League's Second Annual Congress in Syracuse October 26-27, 1878 on "Morality and Liberty," and joined Wise, Ellinger, and Felsenthal as a Vice-President of the newly reconstituted National Liberal League of America, October 27, 1878.[74] He also seems to have held Abbot in high esteem, for on the occasion of a testimonial dinner honoring Abbot and bidding him farewell as editor of *The Index*, June 24, 1880, Schlesinger sent a telegram which characterized Abbot as a "Hebrew Prophet" whose religion of humanity was most akin to Judaism.[75]

Jewish laymen also joined and heartily endorsed the National Liberal League. At the First Annual Liberal League Congress held in Rochester, N.Y. on October 26-28, 1877, Moses Hays of Rochester announced that he had been accused of being an atheist because he belonged to the League. Not so, he protested; he wanted it known that he was a Jew, that the League was for everyone, and that it worked for the emancipation of all mankind.[76] Other apparent Jewish lay members of the National Liberal League included Henry F. Rothschild, New York City, N. Grossmayer and Morris Einstein, Titusville, Pa.; Isaac Liebman, Atlanta; Louis Lowenthal, Rochester; Alex Rosenspitz, Nashville; Moses Bloom, Iowa City, Iowa, and Joseph Singer, Chicago.[77]

Abbot and Felix Adler

Despite Abbot's interaction on religious and political issues with some of the most eminent Jews of his day, he does not seem to have established really intimate friendships with his Jewish associates. In part, this lack of deep and lasting Jewish friendships reflected a more general problem. Abbot's rigorous intellectualist orientation, combative personality, and willingness to say what he believed regardless of personal consequences, opposition, or hurt feelings alienated religious conservatives, religious liberals, and secularists alike. He was a man one respected for honesty of conviction and integrity of character, but a very hard person to like. This militated against the forging of close bonds with anyone, Jew or non-Jew. Still, close friendships with Jews were made more difficult, no doubt, because of his patrician Brahmin descent as well as his residence in Boston which had few Jewish residents and an intellectually undistinguished Jewish community in the 1870's. The one exception to his lack of really close social ties with Jews was his intense friendship — and that, too, for only a brief time — with Felix Adler.

Abbot first took note of Adler upon the latter's appointment as a part-time faculty member at Cornell University, the first Jew so appointed. Calling Adler "an accomplished scholar," Abbot interpreted the event as another "happy advance against sectarianism."[78] With the inception of the New York Society for Ethical Culture, in the Winter-Spring of 1876-77, the *Index* for the next four years was replete with glowing praise of Adler, his Society and the good works which they had undertaken, written by Abbot himself or reprinted from other news sources.[79]

From the Spring of 1877 through the Winter of 1879, Abbot became one of Adler's most ardent admirers. In a letter to Adler of May 24, 1877, he expressed his "warm brotherly interest in your movement and you," and invited Adler to become a contributing editor of *The Index*.[80] A few months later, Abbot asked Adler to address the Rochester Convention of the National Liberal League meeting October 26-28, 1877 on "Compulsory Education as a National Necessity under Universal Suffrage," an invitation Adler declined.[81] But Adler reciprocated these invitations, and arranged for Abbot to address his Ethical Culture Society in March 1878 and February 1879.[82] Between 1877 and 1879, Abbot also rose to defend Adler from various Jewish and non-Jewish attacks, including the heated denunciations of him by leading Jews such as Kaufmann Kohler and Isaac M. Wise.[83] By 1879, Abbot's sentiment of deep admiration and affection for Adler reached its peak. He wrote to Adler of his "positive hunger for a long, quiet, private talk" with him and of his "deep sympathy" for him and his practical work.[84] He confided in Adler that he had "learned to love you truly,"[85] and urged Adler to stay with him at his Boston home during the May, 1879 F.R.A. convention: "The hope of a little soul-talk with you at odd hours is full of delight for me, for I am personally drawn towards you, despite your unconcern for some things that deeply interest me! What business had you to get into my head so irresistibly without warnings?"[86]

It is not difficult to discern the reasons for Abbot's enchantment with Adler. He perceived in Adler's departure from Judaism an exact parallel to that of his own passing out of Christianity, and accepted it as further substantiation of his faith in the progress of religious liberalism. Like Abbot, Adler had found his religious background too restrictive and narrow, and had transcended his religious roots in search of a broader social-religious fellowship. Abbot therefore sensed a truly profound religious soul-mate in the person of Adler. Furthermore, the appearance of the Ethical Culture Society, a Jewish society eschewing Judaism in favor of a truly universal religious fellowship as Abbot understood it, seemed to fulfill his most earnest hopes for Judaism. And, perhaps most significantly, by permitting free religious expression, by espousing a coherent moral-religious philosophy (Adler's), and by dedicating itself to practical social activities, the New York Society for Ethical Culture seemed to exemplify and actualize Abbot's fondest ideals. To Abbot, this Society represented what the F.R.A. should have become. Throughout the 1870's Abbot regularly and unsuccessfully appealed to the rest of the F.R.A. leadership to create a unified F.R.A. philosophy and to involve the association in practical social activism. He was repeatedly frustrated.[87] Indeed, at the very time Abbot was beginning to despair of the future of free religion,[88] Adler, a powerful orator, thinker and robust energizer of men, appeared on the scene with a dynamic new Society; and, about the same time Abbot seemed to give up on the F.R.A., Adler became its second President in May 1878. Abbot was thrilled.

On May 24, 1877, Abbot therefore wrote Adler that "you seem to have taken a position respecting Judaism very analogous to that I took respecting Christianity in 1868 — that is, a frank advance from the limitations of all *special historical religions* to the freedom of *universal spiritual* religion. ... We who stand avowedly outside the circle of the world's established religious fellowships may yet be brothers on the broader ground of truth and of our common humanity."[89] Almost two years later, Abbot candidly revealed to Adler in a letter of January 22, 1879 that he and the Ethical Culture Society were "realizing my ten-years old ideal." The Society of Ethical Culture "marvellously well performs the functions of a true Society of Free Religion," Abbot declared, and he should know, since "I am best fitted by my experience to comprehend and appreciate your position as a come-outer from Judaism, being myself a come-outer from Christianity."[90]

One month later, on February 20, 1879, in a front page comment in *The Index* rejecting Rabbi Felsenthal's call to Adler to keep his Society within a denationalized Judaism, Abbot made public these feelings he had expressed to Adler. Felsenthal's call for a "cosmopolitan Judaism" was quite as unacceptable as any "national Judaism," Abbot averred. Past historical religions and the religion of the future were simply irreconcilable, and the "sacrifice of the special traditional tie is in every case inevitable." "The reason why we feel so profound an interest in Professor Adler's Society," Abbot informed his readers, was "precisely because he and they comprehend the inexorable necessity of sacrificing the lesser to gain the greater fellowship — because they hear the same high summons to leave the Mother-Judaism which we heard ten years ago to leave the Mother-Christianity, not with bitterness but with inexpressible sadness, as the only way by which the priceless freedom and fellowship in religion can be won at last *for all.*" Abbot declared that "only by such partings can the yearned-for oneness of mankind in spirit and in truth be finally achieved." While it is only a question of time before all old religions die, "the Free Religious Association and the Society for Ethical Culture ... are the pioneers of an innumerable host of organizations whose mighty work shall be to teach the coming generations how to search for truth in freedom, and how to apply it in the spirit of a love that shall be universal indeed."[91]

By the Sping of 1880, however, despite these strong tributes and almost effervescent expectations, Abbot and Adler had a strong and irreversible falling-out. They disagreed on practical organizational matters concerning the F.R.A., Abbot, for example, seeking more centralized control over projected local F.R.A. societies. Abbot was also chagrined with Adler's lack of interest in his American Liberal Union.[92] More importantly, however, Abbot came to understand that he and Adler advocated two fundamentally distinct philosophies of life, which for Abbot at least, placed them irreconcilably at odds with one another.

A lifelong devotee of science and the need to apply the objective scientific method to all aspects of human life and experience, Abbot believed that science was the best guide for the perfection of mankind and that it justified his faith in a personal intelligent Being operating in the universe. He was a "scientific theist" and "scientific realist."[93] Adler, however, was a follower of Kant, and Kantian idealism was "repugnant" to Abbot because of the "despair of the intellect which lies at the bottom of the Kantian system." Abbot argued that Kant was "the chief founder of all our modern agnosticism," because Kant felt "speculative reason could not solve the great questions of "God, freedom, and immortality." But, Abbot maintained, "we believe in the power of the human mind ... to answer every reasonable question ... and "God, freedom, and immortality" are reasonable questions."[94]

Adler, on the other hand, very cognizant of the concrete evils in the world which seemed to controvert Abbot's theistic belief in a moral omnipotent Being, was far less sanguine about the powers of science to yield intellectual certainty on critical issues of religious faith. Moreover, the essence of religious faith did not rest in the belief in the perfectibility of man through the aid of science, as Abbot held, but rather in "the belief that, notwithstanding the evil in the world, there is infinite goodness at heart." On this belief, Adler felt, science had no bearing. He emphasized that one simply could not logically and rationally prove the ultimate triumph of good; nonetheless, "the one thing which religion must give us is the belief in infinite goodness."[95]

In later years the split between the two men unfortunately took on rather rancorous overtones, as Abbot became embroiled in an acrimonious controversy with Josiah Royce over a review the latter had written of his *The Way Out of Agnosticism* in the *International Journal of Ethics* of which Adler was the editor.[96]

In a sense, this cleavage between the two men was somewhat surprising, for their temperament, character, and religious evolution would seem to have made Abbot and Adler unusually well suited for one another. Religious liberals steeped in modern scholarship on religion, both men were irascible, logical extremists, evincing single-minded fidelity to fostering coherence between their actions and beliefs. Neither brooked half-way measures once issues had been clearly defined.[97] Indeed, both men approached issues with the same intellectually idealistic style of thinking and analysis. They both searched for the underlying idea or ideal to explain and define phenomena and having determined and judged it, acted accordingly. Thus, once Abbot judged the central idea of Christianity to be belief in the Messiahship of Jesus, a belief he could not accept, he left Christianity. Similarly, having decided that ethical monotheism was the central core of Judaism, an idea which he could not accept, Adler left Judaism. But it was precisely this single-minded devotion to pursue and develop very specific philosophies of life which helped give helped give rise to their split. Uncompromisingly wedded to different ideals — one might even say passions — Abbot, the "scientific theist" seeking primarily intellectual certainties and Adler, the "Kantian idealist" seeking primarily moral certainties and justifications for moral living, perforce went their own ways.

Conclusion

In rejecting the legitimacy of historical Judaism upon the appearance of Christianity, in summarily dismissing the self-affirmations of Judaism's most modern interpretation at that time — Reform Judaism — and in acclaiming and even glorifying the emergence of a 'Jewish' Society stepping out of Judaism, Francis E. Abbot underscored the basic limits of theological accommodation between Jewish and non-Jewish religious liberals and radicals in the last third of the nineteenth century. Abbot could neither accept nor take seriously the Jews and Judaism on their own Jewish terms.[98] From a vertical historical perspective, moreover, perhaps one might venture to link Abbot's religious universalism which led to his defense of Jews on the one hand but his insistence on their disappearance on the other, to the pattern of other religious universalists, enlighteners, millenarians, and utopians who rose to defend Jews and Judaism but could not accept them as they were. Men like Martin Luther (at first), Abbé Gregiore, Christian Wilhelm Dohm, and groups such as the St. Simonians, some nineteenth century socialists, and some twentieth century communists, among others, come to mind on this score. Universalist ideologies, religious or not, simply do not promote the survival of Jews *as Jews*.

Admittedly, Abbot's vitriolic anti-Christian stance and scientific religious radicalism were not reflective of the mainstream of religious freethinkers, be they identifying Christians or not. Nevertheless, his perception of Judaism and the Jews was quite representative, at the least, of a small number of intellectually influential Unitarians, religious liberals of other denominations, and religious radicals who preached the coming of the "religion of humanity." Whether they deemed this religion "Christian" or not and whether they identified themselves as "Christians" or not, did not change the way they viewed Jews and Judaism, and that view did not substantively differ from that of Abbot. Internal disputes among religious liberals and freethinkers on issues such as "who is a Christian," the meaning of "liberal Christianity," science vs. transcendentalism, and a host of other topics had little relevance to their rather uniform conception of Judaism.[99]

Theology aside, the types of interaction Abbot experienced with Jews also suggest the circumscribed nature of social bonds created by leading Jewish and non-Jewish religious liberals in the post-Civil War era. Social and political issues united them in productive, pragmatic coalition against against commonly recognized foes, especially on the idea of church and state separation and all the practical ramifications engendered by the incomplete application of that doctrine. But, generally speaking, intimate social friendships between Jewish and non-Jewish theologians and intellectuals were not the rule during this period. One must wait for the twentieth century to witness truly close camaraderie such as that between Rabbi Stephen S. Wise and Rev. John Haynes Holmes.

Perhaps the metaphor used by Rabbi Emil G. Hirsch in his caustic strictures against Unitarianism's attitude to the Jew best charactrized Abbot's own approach to Jews and Judaism as well as that of other free religionists:

> For the Catholic, the Jew has been preserved to serve as a living witness to the truth of Christianity; in the opinion of the Protestant, the Jew is the living proof of the curse resting upon him, which the new covenant alone may lift; for the Unitarian, the Jew is an archeological specimen to be properly labelled and put in a glass case, or he is a convenient peg upon which to display one's tolerance ... [For the Unitarian, the Jew] should be content to play the part of an archeological curiosity ...[100]

Except when using the Jews and their experiences as a polemical whip against Christianity, Abbot and other free religionists, Christians or not, consciously or not, often seemed to consider Jews and certainly Judaism to be but "archeological curiosities," or in Toynbee's twentieth century appellation, "fossils." Clearly, the religious rapprochement between distinguished American Jewish and non-Jewish liberal religionists had very decided intellectual and social limits during the last third of the nineteenth century.

FOOTNOTES

*My thanks to the American Jewish Archives for a Marguerite R. Jacobs Fellowship and to the University of Cincinnati's University Research Council for a summer grant which together made this study possible.

[1] Generally speaking, the content of this "religion of humanity" differed from one thinker to the next, and depended on his religious background and bias. Compare, for example, the attitudes of Rabbis Isaac M. Wise and Raphael Lasker who asserted that Judaism would be the universal religion of the future *(Proceedings of the Third Annual Meeting of the Free Religious Association,* May 26, 27, 1870, pp. 58-59 and *Proceedings of the Tenth Annual Meeting of the Free Religious Association,* May 31, June 1, 1877, p. 58, respectively) with those of Rev. S. R. Calthrop, Rev. Henry Blanchard, and Rev. Minot Savage who made the same claim for Unitarianism *(Proceedings of the Seventh Annual Meeting of the Free Religious Association,* May 28, 29, 1874, pp. 31-40, *Proceedings of the Ninth Annual Meeting of the Free Religious Association,* June 1, 2, 1876, pp. 78-86, and *The Index,* June 3, 1880, respectively.) These *Proceedings* will henceforth be referred to as *Proceedings of the F.R.A.*

[2] For a history of the Free Religious Association consult William J. Potter, *The Free Religious Association: Its Twenty Five Years and Their Meaning* (Boston, 1892); Stow Persons, *Free Religion: An American Faith* (Boston, 1947); Sidney Warren, *American Freethought 1860-1914* (New York, 1943), pp. 96-116; J. Wade Caruthers, *Octavius Brooks Frothingham: Gentle Radical* (University, Al., 1977), pp. 98-122; Sidney E. Ahlstrom, "Francis Ellingwood Abbot and the Free Religious Association," *Proceedings of the Unitarian Historical Society,* Vol. 17, Part 2, pp. 1-21; Conrad Wright (ed.), *A Stream of Light* (Boston, 1975), pp. 80-81.

While the F.R.A. platform was open to all, and while, as an organization, it eschewed any specific religious ideology of its own, in practice the F.R.A. was dominated by liberal religionists, especially by the leftist Unitarians and religious radicals who departed from Unitarianism and who were its founders. No Catholic or intellectually middle-of-the road Christian, including more conservative Unitarians, could really feel at home in its midst, certainly not for the first twenty-five years of its existence. The lack of an officially declared ideology did not prevent the F.R.A. from evincing a definite religious and intellectual orientation which — whether transcendentalist or scientific in origin — was suffused with the modern liberal, scholarly currents of the day and decidedly anti-traditional.

Still, the indeterminateness of its ideology fostered ongoing debates as to the character of the F.R.A.: was it to be merely a lecture platform for individuals of different beliefs to share their views with others? Or, was it to represent a coherent religious consensus and understanding — the universal religion to which all aspired? This issue constantly plagued the F.R.A. through the 1870's and was the subject of numerous debates. Cf. for instance, O.B. Frothingham's address, in the *Proceedings of the F.R.A.,* III, May 26, 27, 1870, pp. 10-11.

Jews were especially encouraged to join the F.R.A., and from 1867-1914, a number of Jews, some quite prominent, served on its board and/or participated in the organization's national and local conventions: Isaac M. Wise, Max Lilienthal, Moritz Ellinger, Aaron Guinzburg, Raphael Lasker, S. H. Sonneschein, I. S. Nathans, Henry Gersoni, Judah Wechsler, Felix Adler, Bernhard Felsenthal, Edward Lauterbach, Solomon Schindler, Emil G. Hirsch, William Filene, Charles Fleischer, and Stephen S. Wise.

That Jews were consciously sought out by the F.R.A. leadership to make the Association truly "liberal," not simply a Christian organization, can be seen in remarks by William J. Potter, first secretary of the F.R.A., *Proceedings of the F.R.A.* VII, May 28, 29, pp. 10-11; see too, Potter in *The Index,* January 8, 1870; also, address by Thomas W. Higginson glorifying the F.R.A. as the only organization in which Jews and Christians can speak from the same platform in an atmosphere of tolerance, good will, and mutual respect, *Proceedings of the F.R.A.,* X, May 31, June 1, 1877, p. 86. Indeed, Wise and Lilienthal, the two Reform Jews best known to Christians in the 1860's, were invited to participate in the very first organizational meeting of the F.R.A. held in 1867. Neither could come, but Wise sent his greetings, and was elected one of six Directors of the organization. See *Proceedings of the F.R.A.,* I, May 28, 29, 1868, pp. 117-120.

[3] See Allan Tarshish, "Jew and Christian in a New Society: Some Aspects of Jewish-Christian Relationships in the United States, 1848-1881," *A Bicentennial Festschrift for Jacob Rader Marcus*

(Cincinnati, 1976), pp. 579 and note 52.

⁴The topic of religious interaction between American Jewish and non-Jewish nineteenth century religious liberals — indeed, the entire area of Jewish-Christian relations from an interfaith point of view — has not yet been adequately explored in scholarly research. Salo Baron included this topic in 1949 among the desiderata in American Jewish historical research. That judgment is still relevant today. See Salo W. Baron, "American Jewish History: Problems and Methods," in his *Steeled by Adversity* (Philadelphia 1971), pp. 68-69. This essay was originally an address delivered at the forty-seventh Annual Meeting of the American Jewish Historical Society, February 19, 1949.

⁵On Abbot, see Sidney E. Ahlstrom's unpublished doctoral dissertation for Harvard University, "Francis Ellingwood Abbot: His Education and Active Career," July, 1951; F. A. Christie's article on him in the *Dictionary of American Biography*, (New York, 1937), Vol. I. pp. 11-12; Joseph L. Blau, *Men and Movements in American Philosophy* (New York, 1952), pp. 175-186, in which Abbot is called "a stormy petrel of American intellectual life," p. 175; Herbert W. Schneider, *A History of American Philosophy* (New York, 1963), pp. 281-284.

⁶On the search for Unitarian consensus and the fight over the preamble, see Conrad Wright, "Salute the Arriving Moment," in his *A Stream of Light*, pp. 62-94; also, Persons, pp. 1-41.

⁷The appearance of Free Churches, Independent Liberal Societies, Radical Clubs and local Liberal Leagues in the late 1860's and 1870's reflected the dissatisfaction of some with established Unitarianism and liberal reform. Other examples include C.C. Burleigh's Free Congregational Society at Florence, Mass., Samuel Johnson's Free Church in Lynn, Mass. Thomas W. Higginson's Worcester Free Church in Worcester, Mass., Frothingham's Independent Liberal Church in New York. Felix Adler's New York Society for Ethical Culture represented in large measure the Jewish version of the same phenomenon. Cf. Persons, p. 91, for a list of additional examples; also, see Warren, pp. 30, 102. On Adler, see Benny Kraut, *From Reform Judaism to Ethical Culture: The Religious Evolution of Felix Adler* (Cincinnati, 1979).

⁸Persons, pp. 114-118; Warren, pp. 176-179. On the successful militant Protestant revival in the post-Civil War era and its impact on Jewry see Naomi W. Cohen, "Antisemitism in the Gilded Age: The Jewish View," *Jewish Social Studies*, Summer-Fall, 1979, Vol. XLI, No. 3-4, pp. 191-198; also, Tarshish, pp. 574-579.

⁹Abbot's first contact with Jews may have come in his Unitarian church at Dover, N.H. In 1867, he noted about this situation, "I rejoice especially that several Jews have joined us without, of course, ceasing to be Jews," *Proceedings of the F.R.A.*, I, May 28-29, 1868, p. 76.

¹⁰See Rabbi I. M. Wise's address to the F.R.A. "Permanent and Progressive Elements of Judaism," in *Proceedings of the F.R.A.*, III, May 26, 27, 1870, pp. 83-89; Ellinger's address, *Proceedings of the F.R.A., XI*, May 30-31, 1878, pp. 82-88; Rabbi S. H. Sonneschein's address, *Proceedings of the F.R.A., VII*, May 28-29, 1874, pp. 72-81; Rabbi Aaron Guinzburg's address, *Proceedings of the F.R.A., IV*, June 1-2, 1871, p. 17; Rabbi Raphael Lasker, *Proceedings of the F.R.A., X*, May 31-June 1, 1877, pp. 51-58. See Rabbi Max Lilienthal's address at Boston's Horticultural Hall, on "The Religious Idea in History," published in *The Index*, February 18, 1872; Rabbi Judah Wechsler's address to the New Haven F.R.A. convention, November 8-9, 1877 was also published in *The Index*. November 15. 1877.

¹¹See *The Index*, November 26, 1870 for the publication of Wise's speech at the Toledo F.R.A. convention; April 8, 1871, for the publication of Aaron Guinzburg's essay on "The Essenes Relation to Christianity."

¹²See *The Index*, Sept. 2, 1870, in which Abbot cited Wise's analysis of Christianity and his contention that Jesus never claimed to be the Messiah. Abbot disagreed. See his "What is Christianity," *The Index*, January 8, 1870.

¹³For the sentiments of other liberal and religiously radical Christians on this same theme, see the following: O. B. Frothingham on Judaism — *The Index*, Jan. 8, 1870; *Proceedings of the F.R.A.*, III, May 26, 27, 1870, p. 18 — "Christianity is the crowning glory of religion thus far"; *Proceedings of the F.R.A.*, VII, May 28, 29, 1874, pp. 26-27; William J. Potter on Judaism — *Index*, Jan. 8, 1870; *Index*, March 30, 1872; *Index*, Nov. 26, 1874; *Index*, Sept. 28, 1876; for Unitarians on Judaism, see Rev. Calthrop, *Proceedings of the F.R.A.*, VII, May 28, 29, 1874, p. 35 — "Jesus is the flower of the prophets,"; C.D.B. Mills, *Proceedings of the F.R.A.*, X, May 31, June 1, 1877, p. 65, and *Proceedings of the F.R.A.*, XII, May 29, 30, 1879, pp. 72-73. For an American cultural popularization of this theological stereotype, refer to Michael N. Dobkowski, "American Anti-Semitism: A Reinterpretation," *American Quarterly*, Vol. XXIX, summer 1977, No. 2, p. 168.

¹⁴See Abbot's "Fifty Affirmations," *The Index*, Jan. 1, 1870, perhaps his most succinct formulation of his religious beliefs and approach to religion and religious progress from which he never

wavered. See *Index*, Oct. 25, 1877, in which Abbot asserted that his "Fifty Affirmations" still represented his basic beliefs. Also, Persons, p. 31.

[15]Abbot's "The Genius of Christianity and Free Religion," *The Index*, Jan. 1, 1870, first delivered at Horticultural Hall, Boston, Feb. 14, 1869. Abbot elaborated on Jesus' superiority to Judaism, but then pointed out why Jesus' faith and the Christian's faith in Jesus is thoroughly limited and unacceptable for the modern world.

[16]Abbot's "What is Christianity," *The Index*, Jan. 8, 1870, first delivered at the Unitarian Society of Toledo, July 11, 1869.

[17]"The Hebrew Prophets," *The Index*, March 19, 1870. Emphasis added. Given as lecture to the First Independent Society of Toledo, Nov. 14, 1869.

[18]Kraut, *From Reform Judaism to Ethical Culture*, pp. 218-219.

[19]See his address, *Proceedings of the F.R.A.*, III, May 26, 27, 1870, p. 45.

[20]"Fifty Affirmations," *The Index*, Jan. 1, 1870. For other essays highlighting Abbot's attitude to religion and his faith in the imminence of the universal religion of free religion, see: "The Future of Religious Organization as Affected by the Spirit of the Age," *Proceedings of the F.R.A.*, VI, May 29-30, 1873, pp. 86-94; *The Index*, March 25, 1871; "Genius of Christianity and Free Religion," *The Index*, Jan. 1, 1870; *The Index*, Feb. 14, 1878. His mature thinking, though not changing in substance, is found in his *Scientific Theism* (Boston, 1885) and *The Way Out of Agnosticism* (Boston, 1890). For a good secondary discussion of his scientific theism, see Persons, pp. 31-38, 62-75. See too, Blau, pp. 175-186 and Schneider, pp. 281-284.

[21]*The Index*, March 26, 1870.

[22]For a similar thought, refer to William J. Potter, in *Proceedings of the F.R.A.*, I, May 28-29, 1868, p. 66; "There is a young and progressive Judaism — mingling with the world, abandoning isolating peculiarities of belief and observance, and looking for the advance of Truth as the Messiah that is to come and redeem mankind."

[23]*Proceedings of the F.R.A.*, I, May 28-29, 1868, pp. 108-111. As it happens, Nathans in the 1870s became an apostate from Judaism and became active in the mission movement to New York Jews. Nevertheless, his comments struck the keynote for many of the subsequent addresses on Reform Judaism which Abbot heard.

[24]*Proceedings of the F.R.A.*, I, May 27-28, 1869, pp. 22-23. Abbot called Ellinger's talks "exceedingly broad and catholic in tone," *The Index*, March 19, 1870.

[25]*Proceedings of the F.R.A.*, XI, May 30-31, 1878, pp. 85-88.

[26]"Permanent and Progressive Elements of Judaism," *Proceedings of the F.R.A.*, III, May 26-27, 1870, pp. 83-89.

[27]*Proceedings of the F.R.A.*, VII, May 28-29, 1874, p. 76.

[28]*Ibid.*, p. 79.

[29]Abbot was cognizant of Rabbi Solomon Schindler's activities and lectures in Boston, and reprinted some of his addresses. Cf. Schindler's "Moses and Jews," *The Index*, April 12, 1877; see too on Schindler's denial of a personal Messiah, *The Index*, Nov. 21, 1878. He also reprinted the statement of principles emanating from the Cleveland Rabbinic Conference of 1870. He reprinted as well Rabbi Henry Gersoni's sermon at the laying of the cornerstone of his new Atlanta Temple, May 24, 1875, in which Gersoni asserted that "religious exclusiveness [is] the daughter of religious conceit," *The Index*, July 8, 1875. Abbot occasionally reprinted accounts of American Reform Judaism from other newspapers and expressed distinct approval of and pleasure with any signs of its liberal sentiment or actions. See *The Index*, May 10, 1877, for a reprint of an article on Reform Judaism by the New York *Sun*.

[30]On the exchange of pulpits, see *The Index*, Nov. 12, 1874, Dec. 3, 1874, Feb. 17, 1876, July 17, 1879, and Dec. 18, 1879.

[31]Kraut, *From Reform Judaism to Ethical Culture*, pp. 81-82, 218-219.

[32]*Proceedings of the F.R.A.*, II, May 27, 28, 1869, p. 23.

[33]I. M. Wise, "Outlines of Judaism," *Ibid.*, pp. 116-117. Emphasis is Wise's. One year later, Wise announced that Judaism is a free religious association, and no doubt tongue in cheek, suggested that perhaps he was therefore entitled to be President of the F.R.A. Cf. *Proceedings of the F.R.A.*, III May 26, 27, 1870, p. 87. On the centrality of the Decalogue, see the *Israelite*, May 21, 1869, Aug. 9, 1872, Nov. 5, 1875.

[34]*Proceedings of the F.R.A.*, X, May 31, June 1, 1877, pp. 58-59.

[35]*Proceedings of the F.R.A.*, XII, May 29, 30, 1879, p. 59.

[36]*The Index*, March 19, 1870. Abbot was very happy to cite Ellinger's denial of Jewish nationality. See *The Index*, Sept. 3, 1870. As the years passed, Ellinger and Abbot developed mutual respect for one another which they expressed in their newspapers. Intellectually, Ellinger came as close

to Abbot's position as possible without leaving Judaism, as Felix Adler did. See *Jewish Times*, Dec. 21, 1871, Feb. 23, 1872, Aug. 29, 1873, Oct. 17, 1873; See *The Index*, April 23, 1874, May 7, 1874, June 20, 1878.

[37]*The Index*, Dec. 18, 1873. Wise's remarks were published in the *Israelite*, Nov. 14, 1873, and were prompted by an October speech of Octavius B. Frothingham detailing what the religion of the future would *not* be. Wise, in response, sketched his belief of what it would be. Note that Abbot himself did not refrain from asserting what the name and form of the future religion would be — free religion.

[38]*The Index*, Sept. 18, 1873. Emphasis added. Abbot reported on annual meetings of the U.A.H.C. See *The Index*, Aug. 13, 1874, and Aug. 2, 1877.

[39]Kraut, *From Reform Judaism to Ethical Culture*, pp. 153-171.

[40]*The Index*, May 16, 1878. Emphasis his. See Frothingham's similar challenge to New York's Temple Emanu-El to be a society of pure theists, neither Jewish nor Christian. *The Index*, April 5, 1873. See Rabbi M. Schlesinger's reply that Judaism is pure theism and really is a free religious association. *Jewish Times*, April 11, 1873.

[41]See Abbot's address in the *Proceedings of the F.R.A.*, I, 1868, pp. 75-80, and his address in the *Proceedings of the F.R.A.*, II, 1869, pp. 31-36.

[42]*The Index*, Jan. 8, 1870. Denying this belief meant for Abbot abjuring Christianity.

[43]See the *Proceedings of the F.R.A.*, III, May 26, 27, 1870, p. 51 and *The Index*, Jan. 21, 1871 and Nov. 27, 1879. Note that Abbot also railed against Unitarianism and liberal Christians who still affirmed the "Lordship of Christ" even in non-supernatural guise. They too, according to Abbot, were false to freedom. Cf. *The Index*, Nov. 18, 1871. Moreover, with his definition of Christianity, Abbot asserted that "liberal Christianity" was a contradiction in terms since one could not be a Christian while rejecting the Messiahship of Jesus as most liberals did. This onslaught against Christianity made Abbot the most extreme of free religionists, and alienated Potter, Frothingham, Higginson and other radicals of the F.R.A. who regarded themselves to be "non-Christians," rather than "anti-Christians." As "non-Christians," they recognized the positive contribution of Christianity to the world both in the past and, for some people, in the present. Although they felt Christianity would ultimately disappear, they did not feel constrained to remonstrate against it. Abbot characterized proponents of these views as sentimental free religionists in contrast to the intellectual, logically consistent free religionist which he believed he represented. See *Proceedings of the F.R.A.*, VIII, May 27, 28, 1875, pp. 47-58 and *The Index*, Feb. 20, 1879. From time to time, Abbot was rebuked within the F.R.A. for his anti-Christianity. Cf. *Proceedings of the F.R.A.*, VI, May 29, 30, 1873, p. 89 for Lucretia Mott's censure. See too *The Index*, June 1, 1872 for a contrast of Frothingham and Abbot's views of free religion. Consult also Persons, p. 32 ff.

[44]Abbot may well have concurred with Rosemary Ruether's contention that the "left hand of Christology" is inherently anti-Judaic and hence the source of Christian antisemitism. Indeed, his position seems to portray a mirror image of that argument: affirming the historical and contemporary merit of the Jews necessarily resulted in a polemic against Christianity. See Rosemary Ruether, *Faith and Fratricide* (New York, 1974).

This technique of defending Jews as a polemical weapon in internecine Christian conflicts was neither new nor restricted to religious liberals and radicals. Martin Luther, at the outset, castigated the Catholic Church for its treatment of Jews, in part to support his own Christian vision which also foresaw the conversion of the Jews under a more benign policy. In more recent American history, Protestant churches, even conservative ones, evinced pity and support of the Jews in the Mortara Affair of 1858 to flagellate the Catholic Church, "Jesuitism" and "Popery."

[45]*The Index*, Dec. 21, 1876. See the Sunday *Herald*, Dec. 17, 1876. The *Herald's* interpretation of the motivation for this refusal might have been incorrect. The synagogue could have forfeited the money to avoid bad publicity. Social rather than idealistic reasons may have prompted the synagogue action. This issue, however, is extraneous to our concern, which focuses on the use which *The Index* made of the case.

[46]*The Index*, Sept. 4, 1870. Touro, in fact, never owned most of Newport.

[47]*The Index*, Dec. 18, 1873; also, *The Index*, Sept. 18, 1873, and Sept. 25, 1873.

[48]*The Index*, May 31, 1877.

[49]*The Index*, Oct. 16, 1873.

[50]*The Index*, June 25, 1875 and Jan. 10, 1878.

[51]*The Index*, Aug. 13, 1874.

[52]*The Index*, May 21, 1874.

[53]Abbot was not averse to accusing Jews of prejudice when he deemed it appropriate, although such references in *The Index* appear only rarely. See *The Index*, Sept. 25, 1873 in which Abbot called a rabbi a bigot for refusing to swear on a Christian Bible in court. See too *The Index*, Feb. 8, 1877, June 20, 1878, and July 4, 1878 for Abbot's criticism of an English Jewish judge.

[54]On the Seligman-Hilton affair, *The Index*, June 28, 1877. See too his reactions on another occasion of social prejudice based on religious grounds, *The Index*, June 10, 1880. On Marr, see *The Index*, Jan. 29, 1880.

[55]*The Index*, June 21, 1873, Jan. 27, 1876, and Jan. 1, 1880.

[56]*The Index*, April 13, 1877.

[57]*The Index*, Sept. 7, 1873.

[58]Refer to Warren, pp. 176-179 and Persons, pp. 114-118. See too Tarshish, pp. 576-579.

[59]On the issue of non-sectarian Thanksgiving, see Morris U. Schappes, *A Documentary History of the United States* (New York, 1971), pp. 235-246; on Jews and Sunday Laws, see Schappes, pp. 279-280; see the *Israelite*, July 19, 1867, May 25, 1877, May 30, 1879 in which Wise denounced these discriminatory laws. On attempts to insert Christ into the Constitution, see Wise's comments in the *Israelite*, Jan. 18, 1861, Jan. 9, 1863, Feb. 27, 1863, Feb. 18, 1864, July 3, 1868, Feb. 5 and 12, 1869, Feb. 19, 1869, June 4, 1869, Nov. 19, 1869, March 4, 1870, March 11, 1870, March 25, 1870, May 13, 1870, Dec. 15, 1871, Feb. 2 and 9, 1872, March 1, 1872, April 5, 1872. On Jewish opposition to Bible readings in public schools, see *Jewish Times* for Rabbi M. Schlesinger's addresses, June 4, 11, 25, 1875, and July 23, 1875. See Wise's comments in *Proceedings of the F.R.A.*, III. May 26, 27, 1870, pp. 58-59.

[60]See *The Index*, March 25, 1870; see too Schappes, pp. 520-537.

[61]*The Index*, Dec. 2, 1875.

[62]*Ibid.*

[63]*The Index*, Nov. 15, 1876.

[64]*The Index*, Jan. 20, 1872.

[65]*The Index*, May 4, 1876, Dec. 14, 1876, Feb. 22, 1877.

[66]See for example, Ellinger's views in his *Jewish Times*, Feb. 16 and 23, 1872; consult Wise's views, *Israelite*, Feb. 2 and 9, 1872, March 1, 1872, and April 5, 1872. Cf. Persons, p. 117, and Warren, p. 177.

[67]Cf. Abbot's "Nine Demands of Liberalism," platform of the local Leagues, *The Index*, Jan. 4, 1873. Jewish members of local Leagues included N. Grossmayer and Morris Einstein (a self-avowed atheist of Jewish origin) of the Titusville, Pa. League (see *The Index*, Oct. 18, 1877); Rabbi Henry Gersoni of Atlanta, Rabbi Max Schlesinger of Rochester, N.Y., Henry F. Rothschild of New York City, and undoubtedly a good number more. See the Abbot Papers, Harvard University, HUG. 1101.66, Box 4, for a list of local League delegates to the Centennial Congress of Liberals held July 1-4, 1876. On Isaac M. Wise's support for the Leagues, see Ahlstrom's dissertation on Abbot, p. 195.

[68]On the founding of the League, see *The Index*, July, 1876 issues, as well as Oct. 18, 1877. Refer to Persons, pp. 117-118, p. 125; Warren, pp. 35-37, 162-183; Caruthers, p. 131 ff., and ch. 18 of Ahlstrom's unpublished dissertation.

[69]See *The Index*, June 23, 1876 and July 28, 1876.

[70]Letter of Felsenthal to Abbot, May 16, 1876. Abbot Papers, HUG, 1101.66, Box 1, Folder 1. Booth was asked to be a Vice-President, and he accepted in a letter of June 13, 1876. This and all subsequent citations from the Abbot Paper are cited by permission of the Harvard University Archives.

[71]Letter of Wise to Abbot, June 12, 1876, Abbot Papers, HUG. 1101.66, in pamphlet "Extract Letters of Distinguished Citizens," p. 22.

[72]Letter of Ellinger to Abbot, June 19, 1876, Abbot Papers, *ibid.* For Ellinger's interest in the Centennial Congress of Liberals, see the *Jewish Times*, June 23, 1876. He reprinted Abbot's entire address to the National Liberal League, *Jewish Times*, July 28, 1876.

[73]Letter of Gersoni to Abbot, May 14, 1876, Abbot Papers, HUG. 1101.66, Box 2. On Gersoni, see Yaacov Kabakof, *Halutsei ha.-Sifrut Ha-Ivnt Be-Amerika (Tel Aviv, 1966)*, pp. 77-130.

[74]At the Syracuse Conference, the majority of Liberal Leagues voted for a total repeal of Comstock postal laws prohibiting the circulation of obscene literature through the mails. A minority of members, led by Abbot and including eminent Jewish spokesmen, felt that some postal obscenity laws such as those against pornography were legitimate, and that the call for the total repudiation of such laws would seriously misrepresent liberal sentiment in America and also damage the liberal cause. Consequently, this breakaway group founded a new organization with Abbot as President and all officers in the previous organization reappointed to the newly created Nation-

al Liberal League of America. In 1880, this name was changed to the American Liberal Union. Cf. *The Index,* Feb. 12, 1880. See too the letters of Felsenthal, Wise, and Schlesinger consenting to the name change. *Ibid.*

[75] This was not the first time Abbot's religion was likened to Judaism. Henry James, with his notorious loathing of Jews and Judaism, called Abbot's religion "Jewish," — i.e. "selfish and unworldly, as opposed to the greatness of Christianity." *The Index,* Jan. 20, 1876. Abbot responded in that issue, sparking a cycle of correspondence during the next few issues. Cf. *The Index,* Feb. 3 and 17, 1876, March 23, 1876, and May 18, 1876. On James' use of anti-Jewish stereotypes in his literature, such as bourgeois corrupters, materialists, and the like, consult Michael N. Dobkowski, *The Tarnished Dream* (Westport, 1979), pp. 85-88.

[76] *The Index,* Nov. 8, 1877.

[77] Abbot Papers, HUG. 1101.63, book entitled *National Liberal League Centennial Congress, 1876,* pp. 7-30. A large number of other German names appear, some of which may also refer to Jewish individuals, but it was impossible to determine that with any precision. The names included in the text sounded the most Jewish.

[78] *The Index,* April 23, 1874; on Adler at Cornell, refer to Kraut, *From Reform Judaism to Ethical Culture,* pp. 95-107.

[79] Cf. *The Index,* Nov. 30, 1876, Feb. 8, 1877 for praise of Adler; March 1, 1877, the paper cited the praise of Adler of the New York *Sun;* on March 29, 1877, it quoted the *Christian Register* on Adler; on June 21, 1877, and July 12, 1877, it reported on Adler's dismissal from Cornell; on Jan. 24, 1878, it cited the New York *Telegram's* comparison of Adler with Frothingham; on April 4, 1878, it published the bylaws of the New York Society for Ethical Culture; on Adler as new President of the F.R.A., June 13, 1878, June 27, 1878; additional praise of Adler, March 13, 1879, May 15, 1879, May 22, 1879, June 19, 1879, Oct. 23, 1879.

[80] Letter of Abbot to Adler, Abbot Papers, HUG. 1101.8F, vol. 6, p. 47. See too letter of Abbot to Adler on April 21, 1878, *ibid.,* p. 364, in which Abbot assured Adler of his "deep interest in your work and yourself."

[81] Letter of Abbot to Adler, Oct. 4, 1877, Abbot Papers, *ibid.* Adler replied Oct. 16, 1877.

[82] See letters of Adler to Abbot, Feb. 18, 1878; Adler to Abbot, Feb. 22, 1878; Adler to Abbot, March 11, 1878; Adler to Abbot April 8, 1878; Adler to Abbot, Jan. 22, 1879; Abbot to John Frankenheimer, secretary pro-tem of the Ethical Culture Society, Feb. 19, 1879. Abbot Papers, HUG. 1101.8F. Abbot very much enjoyed his experiences at the Society. See too *The Index,* Feb. 6, 1879.

[83] On Kohler-Adler controversy, refer to *The Index,* April 11, 1878 and May 16, 1878; also, consult Kraut, *From Reform Judaism to Ethical Culture,* pp. 158-159. On his critique of Wise, see *The Index,* Feb. 20, 1879. Interestingly, Wise still allied himself to Abbot's National Liberal League of America despite this dispute. See *The Index,* Feb. 12, 1880.

[84] Letter of Abbot to Adler, Jan. 22, 1879, Abbot Papers, *op. cit.*

[85] Letter of Abbot to Adler, April 2, 1879, *ibid.*

[86] Letter of Abbot to Adler, May 15, 1879, *ibid.* No letters of Adler to Abbot expressing such apparently deep emotional attachment are extant. Adler's letters to Abbot express respect, gratitude, common goals, but not compelling personal sentiments. Whether Adler had these feelings, therefore, is not clear. Abbot's reference to Adler's lack of interest in things of deep interest to him probably suggested Adler's unwillingness to involve himself in the political issues of the National Liberal League of America. At this point, Adler was quite skeptical of the ability of "political organizations of any kind" to effect important changes in the religious issues of the day. See letter of Adler to Abbot, Oct. 16, 1877, *ibid.*

[87] See, for example, his address in the *Proceedings of the F.R.A.,* IX, June 1, 2, 1876, pp. 13-14.

[88] Refer, for instance, to his talk in the *Proceedings of the F.R.A.,* XII, May 29, 30, 1879, pp. 58-64; also, Caruthers, p. 121 ff.

[89] Abbot Papers, HUG. 1101.8F. Emphasis is Abbot's.

[90] *Ibid.*

[91] *The Index,* Feb. 20, 1879. On Felsenthal's call to Adler, see Kraut, *From Reform Judaism to Ethical Culture,* pp. 161-165.

[92] Cf. *The Index,* Jan. 29, 1880 and July 1, 1880 on new activities and departures projected for the F.R.A. See too on the differences between Adler and Abbot, Ahlstrom's thesis, p. 308 fn. 1.

[93] See his attitudes in *Proceedings of the F.R.A.,* VI, May 29, 30, 1873, pp. 86-94; *Proceedings of the F.R.A.,* XII, May 29, 30, 1879, pp. 58-64. See his *Scientific Theism* (1885) and *The Way Out of Agnosticism* (1890), and Blau, pp. 175-186, and Schneider, pp. 281-284.

[94] *The Index,* June 3, 1880.

⁹⁵*The Index*, July 8, 1880. This represented Adler's response to Abbot at the thirteenth F.R.A. annual meeting, May 27, 28, 1880.

⁹⁶In 1888, Abbot replaced Royce at Harvard for one year, and later condensed his lectures into a book, *The Way Out of Agnosticism* (1890). Royce wrote a blistering review of it in the *International Journal of Ethics*, Oct. 1890, pp. 98-113. In the ensuing furor, Abbot claimed that he was libeled, and he wrote the Harvard Board of Trustees seeking redress. The whole episode involving letters and counter-letters by C. S. Pierce supporting Abbot and William James supporting Royce can be found in *The Nation*, Nov. 12, 1891, p. 372, Nov. 19, 1891, p. 390, Nov. 26, 1891, p. 408, and Dec. 3, 1891, p. 426. Adler, a close friend of Royce, was involved in the decision not to publish Abbot's rejoinder to Royce in the *International Journal of Ethics*.

⁹⁷In his diary entry of April 31, 1879, Abbot related how he explained the "key" to his life to his son Everett: "I told him the key to all my public and private life, with all its struggles, was the desire and resolve to live out my highest moral ideal in *logical consistency* with all its requirements, even in details seemingly trivial — to square action with thought, and apply religion to conduct logically." Cited in Ahlstrom's thesis, p. 348. Adler could have written the exact same text. On Adler's demand for logical consistency, see Kraut, *From Reform Judaism to Ethical Culture*, passim.

⁹⁸In the twentieth century, in fact, a major thrust of Christian theology on the Jews concerns the quest for a theological orientation accepting the simultaneous legitimacy of both Jewish and Christian religious claims. See, for examples, Ruether, *Faith and Fratricide;* A. Roy Eckardt, *Your People, My People* (New York, 1974). Alan T. Davies, *Anti-Semitism and the Christian Mind* (New York, 1969); Franklin H. Littell, "Have Jews and Christians a Common Future?" in James E. Wood (ed.), *Jewish-Christian Relations in Today's World*. (Waco, 1971), pp. 125-137.

⁹⁹The attitudes to Jews and Judaism of such "non-Christian" free religionists such as Frothingham, Potter, Higginson, Ednah Dow Cheney, Samuel Johnson, and such intellectually and theologically diverse Unitarians as James Freeman Clarke, Henry Blanchard, S. R. Calthrop, and Minot Savage are remarkably similar. Clarke, in fact, adopted rather negative stereotypes of Judaism as narrow, stifling and oppressive in his work of religious fiction, *Legend of Thomas didymus, the Jewish Sceptic*. See Dobkowski, *The Tarnished Dream*, pp. 16-17.

¹⁰⁰Cited from the *Reform Advocate* by the *American Israelite*, Aug. 22, 1895.

Contributors

Elinor Grumet received her doctorate from the University of Iowa. She is currently a Mellon Post-Doctoral Research and Teaching Fellow in the Department of Religion, Brown University, Providence, Rhode Island.

Franklin Jonas received his doctorate from New York University. He teaches at Long Island University and the New York Institute of Technology. Dr. Jonas is co-author of *Urban Legacy: The Story of America's Cities* (New York, 1977).

Ian Bickerton received his doctorate from the Claremont Graduate School, California. He is Senior Lecturer in American History at the University of New South Wales, Australia. His latest article, "Harry S. Truman, the Cold War and the Foundation of Israel" will appear in a forthcoming volume entitled *Harry S. Truman, Man and Statesman,* edited by Allen Weinstein.

Louis Schmier received his doctorate from the University of North Carolina at Chapel Hill. He is Professor of History at Valdosta State College, Georgia. Dr. Schmier has published a number of articles on Southern Jewish history.

Norma Fain Pratt received her doctorate from UCLA. She is Professor of History at Mt. San Antonio College, California and is currently Visiting Professor of History at Sarah Lawrence College, Bronxville, N.Y. Dr. Pratt is the author of *Morris Hillquit: A Political History of An American Jewish Socialist* (Westport, Connecticut, 1979).

Benny Kraut received his doctorate from Brandeis University. He is Associate Professor and Director of the Judaic Studies Program at the University of Cincinnati, Ohio. Dr. Kraut is the author of *From Reform Judaism to Ethical Culture: The Religious Evolution of Felix Adler* (Cincinnati, 1979).

American Jewish Archives Fellowship Programs

The American Jewish Archives sponsors four annual fellowship programs. *The Rabbi Harvey B. Franklin Memorial Award in American Jewish History* is available to ABD's for two months of active research or writing at the American Jewish Archives during the academic year, October to June. The stipend is $1,000 and the application deadline is December 31. *The Marguerite R. Jacobs Memorial Post-Doctoral Award in American Jewish History* is available for postdoctoral candidates for two months of active research or writing at the American Jewish Archives between the months of June and August. The stipend is $2,000 and the application deadline is December 31. *The Loewenstein-Wiener Summer Fellowship Awards in American Jewish History* are available to ABD's or postdoctoral candidates for one month of summer research or writing at the American Jewish Archives. The stipend is $500 for ABD's and $1,000 for postdoctoral candidates and the deadline for applications is December 31. *The Bernard and Audre Rapoport Fellowship in American Jewish History* is available to postdoctoral candidates for research or writing at the American Jewish Archives for a three-month period during the academic year, October to June. The stipend is $3,000. Application deadline is April 1, of the preceding academic year. For more information write to the Director of the American Jewish Archives, 3101 Clifton Avenue, Cincinnati, Ohio 45220.

Fellows of the American Jewish Archives
1977-1981

1977
Loewenstein-Wiener Fellow
Jonathan Sarna, Yale University
"A Biography of Mordecai Manuel Noah"

1978
Loewenstein-Wiener Fellow
Robert Shapiro, Harvard University
"A Biography of Rabbi Stephen S. Wise"

1979-1980
Bernard and Audre Rapoport Fellow
Jonathan Sarna, HUC-JIR
"A History of American Attempts to Convert Jews"

Loewenstein-Wiener Fellow
Ian Bickerton, University of New South Wales, Australia
"American Presidential Policy Towards Israel, 1945-1970"

Marguerite R. Jacobs Post-Doctoral Fellows
Franklin Jonas, Long Island University
"A Biography of B. Charney Vladeck"

Benny Kraut, University of Cincinnati
"The Relationship of the American Free Religious Association and Liberal Judaism"

Ellen Messer, Yale University
"Reform Judaism as a Religion: An Anthropological Perspective"

Norma Fain Pratt, Mt. San Antonio College (California)
"Women's Issues: A Content and Comparative Analysis of the Immigrant and American Jewish Press, 1914-1920"

Louis Schmier, Valdosta State College (Georgia)
"Lost Generations: A Biography of a Southern Jewish Community, Valdosta, Georgia"

Rabbi H. B. Franklin Fellows
   Mark Cowett, University of Cincinnati
   "Rabbi Morris Newfield: A Biography"

   Mitchell Gelfand, Carnegie-Mellon University
   "Social Mobility of the Jews in Los Angeles, 1900-1940"

   Elinor Grumet, University of Iowa
   "The Menorah Journal: A History"

   Stephen Mostov, Brandeis University
   "A Social History of Cincinnati Jewry, 1840-1875"

   Robert Rockaway, Tel-Aviv University
   "The Jews of Detroit: A History"

   Ida Cohen Selavan, University of Pittsburgh
   "Jewish Cultural Activities in Pittsburgh: A History"

1980-1981

Bernard and Audre Rapoport Fellow
   William Toll, University of Oregon
   "American Cultural Pluralism: A Black and Jewish Perspective"

Loewenstein-Wiener Fellow
   Benny Kraut, University of Cincinnati
   "Liberal Jews and Christians in Post-Civil War America"

Marguerite R. Jacobs Post-Doctoral Fellow
   Judith Laikin Elkin, Albion College (Michigan)
   "Latin American Jewish Studies"

Rabbi H. B. Franklin Fellows
   Ellen Sue Elwell, University of Indiana
   "A History of the National Council of Jewish Women"

   Evyatar Friesel, Hebrew University of Jerusalem
   "Early Zionism and the Reform Movement in America"

   Thomas Kolsky, George Washington University
   "The American Council for Judaism: an Anti-Zionist Organization, 1943-1968"

   Michael Leigh, London University
   "Conservative Judaism in Great Britain"

   David Prudson, Tel-Aviv University
   "The American Communist Party and the Jewish Labor Movement, 1919-1929"

INDEX

A

ABBELL, MAXWELL, 58
ABBOT, EVERETT, 113n.97
ABBOT, FRANCIS ELLINGWOOD, 90-113
ACW, see Amalgamated Clothing Workers
ADAMS, SHERMAN, 60
ADLER, FELIX, 91, 97, 102, 103, 104-105, 107n.2, 108n.7, 110n.36, 112n.86, 113n.96, 113n.97
Agnosticism, 104
Agriculture, see Farming, farmers
Albany, Georgia, 64, 69-71, 72, 74, 75
Albany Chapter #15, Royal Arch Masons, Albany, Georgia, 70-71
Albany Hebrew Congregation, 64, 70, 72, 74
Albany Masonic Lodge #24, Albany, Georgia, 70-71, 72, 75
Algeria, 52
"All-rightniks," 33
Amalgamated Clothing Workers, 81, 85
American Israelite, 18
America, see United States
American Hebrew, The, 17, 57
Americanization, see Assimilation
American Jewish Committee, 39
American Jewish Conference, 51
American Jewish Congress, 39, 54
American Jews, American Jewry, 22n.3, 47-48, 49, 50, 51, 52, 53, 57, 58-59, 60, 61, 90, 91, 93, 97, 98, 99-101, 102, 106, 107n2; Eastern European Immigrants, 78-89; Southern, 10, 64-77
American Labor Party, 40
American Liberal Union, 104, 111n.74
  see also National Liberal League of America
American Mercury, 12
American Reform Judaism, 72-73, 94, 97. See also Reform Judaism
"Ancient Jewess and Modern Ones, The," 84-85
Anglo-Iranian Oil Company, 50
Anglo-Jewish Press, 93
Anti-Christian, 92, 96, 98, 100, 105, 110n.43
Anti-Jewish, 96
Anti-Semitism, 11-12, 15, 18, 28, 39, 49, 51, 52, 71, 85, 97, 98, 99, 100, 110n.44. See also Bigotry
APTHEKER, ESTHER, 79-80
Arabists, 49
Arab policies, United States, 47, 50, 60
  See also Middle East policy
Arabs, 52
ARENDT, HANNAH, 14
Ari, legends of, 16
Army, United States, 56, 57. See also Military, United States
Art, artists, 16, 85
Artisans, 27, 80

ASCH, SHOLOM, 29
Assassinations, Russian, 27-28
Assimilation (Americanization), 33-34, 36, 37, 40, 66, 67-68, 69, 74, 81, 83-84, 85, 87. See also Jewish-Gentile relations
Atheism, 101
Atlanta, Georgia, 69, 71, 72
Atlanta Constitution, 75
Atlanta Temple, Atlanta, Georgia, 109n.29
Authoritarianism, religious, 91, 92, 98

B

BALBONI, ALAN, 47
Balkan question, 38
BARON, SALO, 14, 23n.14
Barton Academy, Mobile, Alabama, 22n.3
Battery Harris, 64
BAUER (BAUR), FERDINAND CHRISTIAN, 93
BELASCO, DAVID, 18
Beliefs, religious, 94, 95, 104, 105, 109n.22
BELL, DANIEL, 27
BELLOW, SAUL, 24n.33
BELOW ZERKOW, Russia, 19
BEN-GURION, DAVID, 51
BERG, LOUIS, 12, 13, 14-15, 16, 20
BERG, MOE, 19
BERGELSON, DAVID, 15
BERLIN, ELLIN (né:MacKay), 18
BERLIN, IRVING, 18
Bialystok, Poland, pogrom, 80
Bible, 9, 10, 19, 92, 93, 94, 95, 96, 99, 100, 111n.53
Biblical forefathers, 74
Bigotry, see Religious tolerance
BILLIKOPF, JACOB, 53
Biro-Bidzhan proposal, 15
BLANCHARD, REV. HENRY, 107n.1, 113n.99
BLAU, RABBI JOEL
BLOCH, CHAIM, 16
BLOCH, J.G., 98
BLOOM, MOSES, 101
Blue Laws, see Sunday Blue Laws
B'nai B'rith, 57, 72, 73, 75; District Grand Lodge No. 7, 19
B'nai B'rith Messenger, 82
BODENHEIM, MAXWELL, 13
Bolshevism, 29, 40
BOOTH, Judge, 100, 111n.70
Boston, Massachusetts, 91, 101, 102
Boston Advocate, 18
Bourgeois values, Jewish, 18
BOURNE, RANDOLPH, 11, 20
Boyle Heights, Los Angeles, 80

Bread Upon the Waters, 81
Britain, Great, 49, 50, 51, 52; Jews, 98
BROOKE, TUCKER, 11
Brooklyn, New York, 15, 38, 40-41. *See also* East Side, New York City
Broom, 12
Brotherhood, Jewish, 73, 74, 85
BROWNE, RABBI EDWARD B., 71-73
BUBER, MARTIN, 16
Bund, the, *see* Jewish Labor Bund
Burleigh, C.C., 108n.7
Business, business people, 10, 27, 69, 71, 73, 74, 80, 85

C

Cafe Royale, New York City, 13
CAHAN, ABRAHAM, 37, 38, 40
California, 79. *See also* Los Angeles
California Jewish Review, 83
California yidisher shtime, 85
CALTHROP, REV. S.R., 107n.1, 113n.99
CANBY, HENRY SEIDEL, 19-20, 23n.8
CASTELAR, EMILIO, 98
Catholicism, Catholics, 106, 107n.2, 110n.44
Centennial Congress of Liberals, 100
Charity, charities, 27, 68, 70, 74. *See also* Philanthropy, Jewish; Social work; War relief
Charleston, South Carolina, 69
CHARNEY, BARUCH NACHMAN, see Vladeck, Baruch Charney
CHARNEY, DANIEL, *see* Tcharney, Daniel
CHARNEY family, 27; Samuel, 27, 28, 29-30, 41n.6; Wolf, 27
CHENEY, EDNA DOW, 113n.99
Chicago, Illinois, 30; public schools, 99, 100
Child abuse and neglect, 89n.21
Children, Jewish, 79, 80, 81-82, 83, 84, 87, 88n.13, 88n.14, 89n.21
CHRIST, *see* Jesus, Christ
"Christian Amendment," 92, 99, 100
Christianity, Christians, 67, 68, 90, 91, 92, 93, 94, 95, 96, 97, 98, 99, 100, 102, 103, 105, 106, 107n.2, 108n.12, 109n.15, 110n.40, 110n.42, 110n.43, 110n.44, 111n.53, 113n.98, 113n.99. *See also* Gentiles; Unitarianism, unitarians.
Christian press, 93
"Chronicles," *Menorah Journal*, 15, 24n.16
Church, Christian, 92, 97, 98, 100
Church and state separation, 92, 98, 99, 100, 106
Cincinnati, Ohio, 73; public schools, 99
Citizenship, 34, 36, 68, 70, 71, 98
City of Hope, 85
Civic affairs, 69, 70-71
Civil War, American, 68-69
CLARKE, JAMES FREEMAN, 113n.99
CLAY, LUCIUS, 58
Clergy, Christian, 90, 91, 98. *See also* Rabbis
Clerical work, clerks, 80, 82, 85, 87
Cleveland Rabbinic Conference of 1870, 109n.29
COHEN, ELLIOT, 8-25
COHEN family (GABALSKY), 9-10; ANNETTE (ROBINSON), 22n.5; ELSA RUTH (HERRON), 22n.5; HARRY 9-10, 22n.2; MANDEL, 9, 10-11; 22n.5; MYRA, 22n.5; REUBEN, 21; ROSA (ROSE), 9, 10; SYLVIA (né: KANTROWITZ), 10, 22n.4; TOM ELLIOT, 22n.4
College education, 81, 83
Columbia University, 58
"Commentaries," *Menorah Journal*, 14-15, 17, 24n.15
Commentary, 9, 13, 14, 20, 14n.15
Commercial enterprises, *see* Business, business people
Communes, Jewish, 85
Communications industry, 48
Communists, 85, 89n.23, 105
Communities, Jewish, 27-29, 65-66; American, 9, 14, 15, 16, 17-19, 21, 26, 30, 38, 47, 48, 49, 50, 53, 58, 93, Boston, 102, Los Angeles, 78-89, New York City, 39, Southern, 10, 69-70, 71, 72, 73-75.
Comparative religion, 92
Comstock postal laws, 111n.74
Concentration camps, 52; Nazi, 51, 53, 55, 57, 60, 62n.23
Confederate Army, 64, 65, 69
Congregations, Hebrew, 97
Congress, United States, 47, 49, 53, 57, 62n.23, 92, 99, 100
Conscience, 96
Conservative Judaism, 84, 85
Constitution, United States, 92, 99
Conversion movements, 99, 109n.23, 110n.44
Cornell University, 102
"Cosmopolitan Judaism," 103
Covenant, 94, 106
Creeds, religious, 92, 94, 95
Crusade in Europe, 54
Cry for Justice, The, 37
Culture, Jewish, *see* Identity, Jewish; Yiddish culture
Culture, popular, 19, 29-30, 74
Czarist Russia, 10, 27-28, 29, 30, 31, 32, 36, 37, 41n.4, 41n.14, 86

D

DAHLBERG, EDWARD, 13
DALLAS, GEORGIA, 69
Daniel Deronda, 9
DANTE, ALIGHIERI, 19
DARLAN, JEAN FRANCOIS, 52
Darwinism, 92
DAVIS, SADIE GORTATOWSKY, 66-67, 68, 70, 75
Decalogue, 96
Defense Department, United States, 49
Del Pezzo's, New York City, 16
Democratic party, Democrats, 47-48, 50, 51, 61
Denver, Colorado, 58
Depression, the, 79
Deproletarianization, 81
Der Arbeiter, 30
Dial, 12
DIAMOND, JOSEPH, 18
DIAMOND, "WHITEY", 18
Di Naye Tsayt, 29
Discrimination, *see* Religious tolerance
Displaced Persons, 51, 53-55, 56-58, 61

DISRAELI, BENJAMIN, 98
Di Zukunft, 30
Dogma, religious, 92, 94, 96, 98
DOHM, CHRISTIAN WILHELM, 105
Domestic service, 80, 82
Dougherty County, Georgia, 64, 71
Dover, New Hampshire, 91
DUBINSKY, DAVID, 40
Dukor, Lithuania, 27
DULLES, JOHN FOSTER, 47, 49, 50-51
Duma elections (Russian), 28

E

East, the (United States), 79, 80; 85
Eastern Europe, 80. See also Eastern European Jews; Hungary; Lithuania; Poland; Prussia; Rumania
Eastern European Jews, 27, 28, 29, 30, 36, 38-39; United States Immigrants, 78-89. See also Hungarian Jews; Lithuanian Jews; Polish Jews; Prussian Jews; Rumanian Jews
East Side, New York City 39; Lower, 12-13, 32, 40
"Eating days," 27
EBAN, ABBA, 50, 58
Editing, editors, 8-25, 29, 36-37, 62n.23, 71, 92
EDMAN, IRWIN, 13, 21
Education, 11-12, 19-20, 28, 68, 72, 73, 91, 93, 102, 113n.96; compulsory, 102; Jewish women, 78, 81, 82, 83-84, 85, 86, 87, 88n.13. See also Religious education; Students; Teachers
Egypt, 49, 50
EINSTEIN, MORRIS, 101, 111n.67
EISENHOWER, DWIGHT D., 47-63
EISENHOWER, JOHN, 48-49
"Elder of Zion, An," 17
ELLINGER, MORITZ, 93, 95, 96-97, 100, 101, 107n.2, 109, 110n.36
ELIOT, GEORGE, 9
Emotionally disturbed children, 88n.14, 89n.21
Employers' Association, Los Angeles, California, 82
England, see Britain, Great
English Jews, 98
English language, 14, 15, 33, 34, 66, 67, 68, 84
Equal rights, 39, 72, 74, 85-86, 97. See also Religious freedom
Ethical Culture Society, see New York Society for Ethical Culture
Ethics, Judaic, 18, 68, 71, 72. See also Moral virtue.
Ethnic identity, ethnic groups, 46, 48. See also identity, Jewish.
ETTELSON, SAMUEL AARON, 9, 22n.2
Europe, 51, 53, 56, 57, 58, 60, 79. See also Eastern Europe
European Jews, 51, 53-55, 56-57, 60, 97; literature, 15-16. See also Eastern European Jews; English Jews, German Jews
European relief, see War relief
European scholarship, 92
Externs, Jewish, 28
Evil vs. good, 104
Evolution, theory of, 92, 94
Extermination camps, see Concentration Camps, Nazi

F

FADIMAN, CLIFTON, 14, 16, 17, 23n.14
Faith, religious, 95, 96, 97, 104
Families, Jewish immigrant, 79, 80-81, 82, 83-85, 86-87
Farming, farmers, 67, 68, 73-74
Fascist party, Italy, 18
Fathers, Jewish, 79, 81, 83, 85, 86, 87
FEARING, KENNETH, 13
Federation for the Support of Jewish Philanthropic Societys of the New York City, 44n.110
Feldafing camp, 53, 56-57
FELSENTHAL, RABBI BERNHARD, 99, 100, 101, 103, 107n.2
Feminine roles, 84-86, 87
Feuchtwanger, Lion, 16
FILENE, WILLIAM, 107n.2
FINEMAN, IRVING, 13
First World War, 10, 15, 26, 36, 37, 39, 44n.110
FISHER, MORRIS, 19
FLEISCHER, CHARLES, 107n.2
Foreigners, Jews as, 65
Foreign policy, United States, 46, 47, 49-51, 52, 53, 54-55, 56, 57, 59, 60, 61, 62n.23
Fort Sumter, 68
Forverts, 34, 35, 37
Forward, see *Jewish Daily Forward*
Forward Association, 30
F.R.A., see Free Religious Association
France, 49
Fraternal lodges, 73, 74
Free Church, Lynn, Massachusetts, 108n.7
Free-church movement, 92, 108n.7
Free Congregational Society, Florence, Massachusetts, 108n.7
Freedom, political, 66, 74, 85-85, See also religious freedom
"Free religion," see Freethought, religious
Free Religious Association, 91, 92, 93, 95-96, 99, 100, 103, 104, 107n.2, 109n.33, 110n.33
Freethought, religious, 90, 91, 92, 93, 94-97, 98, 100, 102-103, 104-106, 107n.1, 107n.2, 109n.33, 110n.37, 110n.40, 110n.43, 113n.97, 113n.99
Freiheit, 78
French North Africa, 51, 52
FREUD, SIGMUND, 16
"From the American Scene," *Commentary*, 14
"From the Depth of Our Hearts," 36-37
FROTHINGHAM, OCTAVIUS B., 91, 92, 97, 108n.7, 110n.37, 110n.40, 110n.43, 113n.99

G

GABALSKY family, see Cohen family
GAMBETTA, LEON, 98
Gangsterism, 15
Garment trade unions, 31-32
Garment workers, 78, 80, 81, 82, 85
GARSHUNI, GREGORY, 27-28
GARTNER, LLOYD P., 79
GELFAND, MITCHELL, 81
Gentiles, 83

Georgia, 64, 65, 66, 69-70, 74, 75; farmers, 67, 68; politics, 71, 72
"Georgia Gentiles," 67
Georgia Royal Arch Masons, 64, 70-71, 75
Georgia Volunteers, 64, 65, 69
German Jews, 65; U.S. immigrants, 79, 81, 83
Germany, post war, 51, 53, 54, 55, 56. See also Nazi Germany
GERSONI, RABBI HENRY, 99, 101, 107n.2, 109n.29, 111n.67
GIDEON, MARRANO, 16
GIDEON, SAMPSON, 16
"Girls in Blue," 34
GLAZER, NATHAN, 41
GOD, 36, 95, 96, 104
GOLDING, LOUIS, 16
GOLDMAN, SOLOMON, 24n.24
GOLDSTEIN, RABBI ISRAEL, 55
GOLL, IWAN, 16
Gollub, Prussia, 65, 67
Good and evil, 104
GOMPERS, SAMUEL, 17
GORDON, VERA, 83
GORTATOWSKY, MORRIS, 65, 69
GORTATOWSKY, SADIE, see Davis, Sadie Gortatowsky
Goyim, see Gentiles
Grand Lodge of District No. 5, Georgia, 72
Greater New York Committee for State of Israel Bonds, 59
GREENBERG, CLEMENT, 24n.15
GREENEBAUM, HENRY, 100
Greenwich Village, New York City, 12-13, 85
GREGIORE, ABBE, 105
GROSSMAYER, N., 101, 111n.67
GUEDALLA, PHILLIP, 16
GUINZBURG, AARON, 107n.2

H

Haaretz, 58
Hadassah, 84
HALPER, ALBERT, 13, 14
HAMBURGER family, 81-82; ASHER 78; DAVID A., 82; HANNAH, 78
Hamburger Home for Working Girls, 78, 81, 82, 88n.14
HARRISON, EARL G., 53, 54, 55-56
Harvard College, 91, 93, 113n.96
Hasidism of Lubavitch, 27
HAYS, MOSES, 101
Health, Jewish, 79, 87
Hebrew Benevolent Congregation, Atlanta, Georgia, 71, 72
Hebrew Benevolent Society, 74; Albany, Georgia, 70
Hebrew Bible, 93, 94 See also Bible
Hebrew congregations, 97
Hebrew Immigrant Aid Society, 27
Hebrew language, 19
Hebrew literature, 9
"Hebrew Prophet," 101
Hebrew race, 94
Hebrew teachers, 9

Henry Street settlement, 34
Herald, Sunday, 98, 110n.45
HERRON, ELSA RUTH, see Cohen family
HEYMAN, HARRY, 38
HIAS, See Hebrew Immigrant Aid Society
HIGGINSON, THOMAS W., 107n.2, 108n.7, 110n.43, 113n.99
HILLMAN, SIDNEY, 40
HILLQUIT, MORRIS, 37-38
Hilton Head prison, 69
HIRSCH, RABBI EMIL G., 106, 107n.2
Historical religions, 94-95, 96-97, 103
HITLER, ADOLPH, 60
Holidays, Holy Days, Jewish, 74, 85; High, 18
Holocaust, 51
HOLMES, REV. JOHN HAYNES, 106
HOLTMAN, RACHEL, 78
Home, the Jewish, 80, 85. See also Families, Jewish
Homeland, Jewish, see Palestine
HOOK, SIDNEY, 16
Housekeeping services, 80
House of Representatives, United States, 49
Housewives, 78
HOWE, IRVING, 32, 86, 87
HUFF, EARL, 47
Humanity, religion of, 91
Humor, Jewish, 16-19
Hungarian Jews, 51
Hungary, 51
HURWITZ, HENRY, 11, 12, 13, 14, 15, 16, 17, 21
Husbands, Jewish, 79, 80, 85-86
Hygiene, household, 83

I

Idealism, Kantian, 104, 105
Identity, Jewish, 13, 16, 19, 21, 33-34, 36, 37, 66, 67-68, 69, 73, 74, 75, 84, 85, 86, 87, 105, 108n.9. See also Nationalism, Jewish
Idische Arbeiter Welt, 30
ILGWU, See International Ladies Garment Workers Union
Immigration, Immigrants, Palestinian, 51, 57
Immigration, immigrants, United States, 9-10, 17, 26, 30, 31, 33-34, 36, 40, 41, 58, 66, 73, 75, 78-89; Second generation, 23n.8
Immigration and Naturalization Service, 53
Immigration quota law, 17
Immortality, 104
Independence Day, 37
Independent Liberal Church, New York, New York, 91, 108n.7
Independent Liberal Societies, 108n.7
Index, The, 91, 92, 93, 97, 98, 99, 101, 102, 103, 110n.53
Institutions, religious, 94
Intellectualism, intellectuals, 9, 11, 19, 21, 48, 85-86; religious, 90, 91, 92, 94, 98, 101, 102, 104, 105, 106, 107n.2, 110n.43
Interfaith movement, 91
Intergovernmental Committee on Refugees, 53
Intermarriage, 18, 96
International Journal of Ethics, 104, 113n.96

International Ladies Garment Workers Union, 81, 85
Iran, 50
Islam, 96
Israel, Israelis, 46, 47, 48, 49-51, 58, 59-60, 61. See also Nationalism, Jewish; Zionism, Zionists
Israelite, The, 73, 91, 93, 110n.37
Israelite (Toledo), 18
Italians, 81
IVES, IRVING M., 59

J

JABOTINSKY, VLADIMIR, 15
Jacksonville, Florida, 69
JAMES, HENRY, 112n.75
JAMES, WILLIAM, 113n.96
Jerusalem (Palestine and Israel), 50, 95
"Jesuitism," 110n.44
Jesus, 93, 94; as Christ, 92, 98, 105, 108n.12, 109n.15
Jewish Advance, 93
Jewish Agitation Bureau, 31, 34
Jewish Centers, 18
Jewish-Christian relations, 90, 91, 93-94, 95-103, 105-106, 108n.4. See also Jewish-Gentile relations
Jewish Daily Forward, 26, 30, 31, 34, 37, 38, 40
Jewish General Workers' Union, see Jewish Labor Bund
Jewish-Gentile relations, 57, 67, 68, 69, 70-71, 73, 74, 75. See also Assimilation; Jewish-Christian relations.
Jewish Guardian, 18
Jewish Labor Bund, 26, 28-30, 31, 32, 33, 34, 37, 40, 86
Jewish Labor Committee, 27, 40
Jewish Legion, 15
Jewish Messenger, 93
Jewish Mothers Alliance of the United States, 84
Jewish press, 15, 17, 30, 57, 58, 71, 72-73, 93
Jewish Record, 93
Jewish Socialist Federation, 34-35
Jewish South, The, 71, 72-73, 77n.42, 77n.43
Jewish Theological Seminary of America, 58
Jewish Times, The, 91, 93, 95, 96-97, 99
Jews, the, 18, 21, 28, 33, 37, 52, 67, 93, 94, 97-99, 105-106, 110n.44, 113n.98, 113n.99. See also American Jews; European Jews; Israel, Israelis; Palestinian Jews
"Jews and family solidarity," 85
Jews, Naturalization Bill (1753), 16
John Addison Porter Fellowship (Yale University), 11
Johnson Immigration Restriction Bill, 17
JOHNSON, SAMUEL, 108n.7, 113n.99
Joint Distribution Committee, 15, 27, 39
JONES, MOTHER, 36
JOSEPH LODGE No. 76, Savannah, Georgia, 72
Journalism, see Editing, editors; Press, the
Judaism, 10, 18, 36, 66, 70, 71, 72, 73, 74, 85, 91, 93, 94, 95, 96, 97, 101, 102-103, 105-106, 107n.1, 109n.15, 109n.22, 109n.33, 110n.36, 110n.40, 112n.75. See also Conservatirve Judaism; Orthodox Judaism; Reform Judaism
JUESSEN, E., 100
Juvenile delinquency, 83

K

Kabalist mysticism, 27
Kabbalistische Sagen, 16
KALLEN, HORACE, 12
KANT, IMMANUEL, 104, 105
KANTROWITZ, SYLVIA, see Cohen family
Kashrut certificate, 18
Khalah, 84
KIEVE, ADOLPH, 69
Kikl, Poland, 29
KOHLER, KAUFMANN, 97, 99, 102
Kosher chicken market, 15
Kosher food, 67, 84
KOSITZA, RACHEL ANNA, 80
KRASS, RABBI NATHAN, 18
KRAUSKOPF, RABBI JOSEPH, 101
KRICKUS, RICHARD, 48
KUHN, ARTHUR J., 19
Ku Klux Klan, Alexandria, Louisiana, 19

L

Labor, female, 80-81; manual, 82, 87
Labor movement, labor unions, 17, 26, 28, 29, 30, 31-32, 34, 35, 37, 38, 39, 40, 41, 44n.110, 81, 82
Ladies Aid Society, 74
LA GUARDIA, FIORELLO HENRY, 40
La Guardia coalition, New York City Council, 27
Landowners, see Farming, farmers
LANDSBERG, RABBI MAX, 101
LASKER, RABBI RAPHAEL, 93, 96, 107n.1, 107n.2
LASSALLE, FERDINAND, 29
LAUTERBACH, EDWARD, 107n.2
Law, religious, 70, 71, 94, 95
Law enforcement, 68
LEE, ALGERNON, 35
Legend of Thomas didymus, the Jewish Sceptic, 113n.99
LEHMAN, HERBERT, 39, 40, 58
LENIN, VLADIMIR ILICH, 29
LEONARD, BENNY, 18
LEVIN, MEYER, 14
LEVIN, SHMARYA, 16
LEVINE, IRVING, 19
LEWISOHN, LUDWIG, 12
Liberlism, liberals, 40; press 91, 92. See also Radicals, Jewish; Religious liberalism, liberals; Socialism, Socialists
Liberal Leagues, 100-101, 108n.7, 111n.67, 111n.74
Liberation, women's see Women's rights
Liberator, 12
Liberty, see Freedom, political; Religious freedom
LIEBMAN, ISAAC, 101
LILIENTHAL, ALFRED M., 49
LILIENTHAL, RABBI MAX, 93, 99, 107n.2
LIPPMANN, WALTER, 38
Literacy, 84
Literature, American, 35; Jewish, 8-25; Jewish stereotypes in, 112n.75, 113n.99. See also Yiddish literature
Lithuania, 27, 28, 41n.4
Lithuanian Jews, 27, 28, 41n.4
"Little magazines," 8

Lodz, Poland, 29, 30; jail, 29
Logic and religion, 105, 113n.97
LONDON, MEYER, 32, 37, 38, 39, 40, 41, 44n.110
LORD, the, see God; Jesus, as Christ
Los Angeles, California, Jewish community, 78-89
Los Angeles Board of Education, 84
Los Angeles Conference of Jewish Women's Organizations, 89n.23
Los Angeles Council, Immigrant Aid and Americanization Department, 83-84
Los Angeles Service League, 84
Louisiana, 73. See also New Orleans
LOWENTHAL, LOUIS, 101
LOWENTHAL, MARVIN, 15-16
Luce empire, 12
Lukishki Prison, Vilna, Lithuania, 29
LUTHER, MARTIN, 105, 110n.44

M

Macaulay, Thomas Babington, 20
Maccabean Zion Club, 84
McCarran-Walter Act, 58
MACKAY, ELLIN (Ellin Berlin), 18
Mankind, faith, in, 95
Manual Labor, female, 82, 87
Marietta, Georgia, 69
MARR, WILHELM, 99
Marriage, 85, 86. See also Intermarriage
MARSHALL, GEORGE, C., 53, 56, 62n.23
MARSHALL, LOUIS, 14, 39-40
MARTINEAU, JAMES, 93
MARX, KARL, 36
Masonic lodges, 64, 70-71, 72, 75
Meadville Theological School, Meadville, Pennsylvania, 91, 93
MEDEM, VLADIMIR, 29
Memoirs of a woman from Bialystok, 80
Menorah Journal, 9, 10, 11, 12-13, 14-16, 17-19, 20
"Menorah Mission," 13
Menorah Society (Yale University), 12
Menorah Summer School, 21
Mercantile establishments, merchants, see Business, business people
Messiah, 94, 95, 98, 105, 108n.12, 109n.22, 109n.29, 110n.43. See also Jesus, as Christ
Mexicans, 81
Meyer's Hotel, Hoboken, New Jersey, 16
Meyn lebns veg, 78
Middle class, 33, 34, 81, 86-87
Middle East, 52, 59
Middle East policy, United States, 47, 49, 50
Midrash, 85
Migration, United States, 79
Mikvah, 84
Military, United States, 52, 53-54, 55, 56, 57, 58, 60. See also Confederate Army
Ministers, Christian, 92, 96
Minsk, Russia, 27, 28 Prison, 28
"Mir, froyen." 86
Missionaries, 49
Missionary movements, see Conversion movements
Mississippi, 73
Mobile, Alabama, 9, 10, 22n.2

Modernity, Jewish women, 84-85
Monotheism, 18, 94, 96, 105
Monroe, Louisiana, 74
MONTOR, HENRY, 53
MOODY, DWIGHT, 99
MORAIS, RABBI SABATO, 99
"Morality and Liberty," 101
Moral virtue, 68, 70, 72, 94, 105, 113n.97. See also Ethics, Judaic
MORGANTHAU, HENRY, JR., 53
MORLEY, CHRISTOPHER, 11
MORROW, FELIX (né: Mayrowitz), 13
Mortara Affair of 1858, 110n.44
MOSES, 65
Moslems, 98
Mothers, Jewish, 79, 80-81, 83, 84, 85, 86, 87
Mt. Carmel Cemetery, Queens, New York City, 41
Mysteries, religious, 96
Mysticism, Kabalist, see Kabalist mysticism

N

NADICH, RABBI JUDAH, 52, 54
NATHANS, REV. I.S., 95, 107n.2, 109n.23
National Conference of the United Jewish Appeal, 57
National Conference of Unitarian Churches, 92
National Council of Jewish Women, 83; Children's Bureau Statistics, 89n.21
National interest, United States, 47, 49-50, 60
Nationalism, Jewish, 16, 33, 39, 85, 94, 97, 103, 109n.36. See also Zionism, Zionists
National Liberal League, 92, 93, 100-101, 102; of America, 101, 111n.74, 112n.83, 112n.86, See also American Liberal Union.
National Reform Association, 99
National Republican Convention, 59, 60
National Workmen's Committee, 39
Native Americans, 81
Natural world, 36
Nazi Germany, 51, 54, 60, 62n.23. See also Concentration camps, Nazi
NEEDLE TRADES WORKERS, 78, 80, 81
NEUMANN, EMMANUEL, 49
New England, 91
New Hope Church, Dallas, Georgia, 69
New Orleans, Louisiana, 77n.42
Newport, Rhode Island, 57, 98
New Testament (Bible), 93
New York City, New York, 15, 26, 30, 31-32, 34, 35, 37-38, 39, 40-41, 44n.110, 73, 79-80, 109n.23; Council, 27, 40. See also Brooklyn; East Side; Greenwich Village
New York City Jewish intelligentsia, 9, 10
New York Society for Ethical Culture, 91, 97, 102-103, 104, 108n.7, 112n.82
NIGER, S. (Samuel Charney), 29, 41n.6
NIXON, RICHARD M., 49
North African campaign, 52
North African Jews, 51
"Northern" press, 73
"Notes for a Modern History of the Jews," 17-19

O

Obscene literature laws, 111n.74
Occupations, Jewish immigrant women, 80-81, 82, 83, 84, 86
Office jobs, 81, 82
Oil, Middle East, 50
Oilmen, 49
OKO, ADOLPH, 17
Old Testament (Bible), 19, 96
Open shops, 81, 82
Organized religion, 94, 95, 96-97, 98
Origins of Christianity, The, 93
Orthodox Judaism, 18, 27, 32, 72, 84, 85, 95

P

PAISER, JOHANNA, see Wessolowsky, Johanna
Pale, Russian, 27, 28, 36, 41n.4
Palestine, 15, 47, 50, 51, 55, 57, 58; homeland, 28. See also Israel, Israelis; Jerusalem; Nationalism, Jewish; Zionism, Zionists
Palestinian Jews, refugees, 50
Palestinian press, 15
Pasifik, 85
Patriarchical family, 85
Patriotism, American, 36, 37, 38, 65, 75
Peddling, peddlers, 66-67, 80
People's ORT, 27
People's Relief Movement, 38-39
People's Store, Los Angeles, California, 81-82
PERETZ, Y.L., 29
Perfectability of man, 95, 104
Periodicals, literary, 8-25
Persecution, see Anti-semitism; Religious tolerance
PESOTTA, ROSE, 81
PETACH TIKVAH, 15
PEYROUTON, MARCEL, 52
PHELPS, WILLIAM LYON, 12, 19, 20, 21
Philadelphia, Pennsylvania, 32, 34, 35, 73; public schools, 99
Philanthropy, Jewish, 15, 53. See also Charity, charities; War relief
PIERCE, FREDERICK E., 20, 24n.27
PIERCE, C.S., 113n.96
Pioneers, Jewish women, 79
Pioneer Women, 84
Plantation owners, Jewish, 73-74
Poale Zion, 28
PODHORETZ, NORMAN, 13, 14
Poland, 28, 29, 30, 37, 41n.4, 51, 80
Polish Jews, 28, 29, 37, 41n.4, 51, 80
Politics, English, 98
Politics, local U.S., 15, 71, 72, 78. See also Politics, United States domestic
Politics, radical, 85-86. See also Politics, socialist
Politics, religious, 112n.86. See also Church and State.
Politics, socialist, 26-45. See also Politics, radical
Politics, United States domestic, 46, 48, 49-51, 58-61. See also Foreign policy, United States; Politics, local U.S.
Pollution, air, 79
"Popery," 110n.44

Pornography laws, 111n.74
Postal laws, 111n.74
POTTER, WILLIAM J., 92, 107n.2, 109n.22, 110n.43, 113n.99
Prayers, women's, 84
Pregnancies, unmarried, 83
Prejudice, see Religious tolerance
Preparedness Movement, 38
Presidency, United States, 46, 47, 48-49, 50-52, 53-54, 58-59, 60, 61
Press, the, 15, 17, 26, 30, 57, 58, 62n.23, 71, 78, 85, 91, 92, 93, 97, 98, 99
Press clippings on Jewish life, 17-19
Prisons, Russian, 28, 41n.14
Proceedings (Free Religious Association), 93
Professionals, Jewish immigrant women, 80, 82, 83
Profiteering, 64, 65
Progress, idea of, 92
"Promise of the American Synagogue, The," 12, 23n.8
Prophets, biblical, 94
Protest, public, 99
Protestantism, protestants, 99, 106, 110n.44; Bible, 94
Prussia, 65-66
Prussian Jews, 65-66
Public housing movement, 27
Public schools, 99, 100
Punishment, spiritual, 94
Pursuing the American Dream: White Ethnics and the New Populism, 48

R

Rabbinical students, 9-10, 27-28
Rabbis, 17, 18-19, 32, 52, 64, 70, 71, 93, 96, 100, 101, 109n.29, 111n.53
"Rachel, pretty", 85
Radical clubs, 108n.7
Radical press, 30, 85
Radicals, Jewish, 85-86, 89n.23. See also Liberalism, liberals; Religious liberalism, liberals; Socialism, socialists
Rationalism, religious, 92, 95, 96, 97, 104
Realism, scientific, 104
Red armies, 55
Red scare, 39
Reform Jewish Women, 83
Reform Judaism, 72-73, 83, 84, 85, 93, 94, 95, 96, 97, 105, 109n.23
Reform Sinai Temple, Los Angeles, California, 84-85
Refugees, War (Jewish), see Displaced Persons
Relief movement (European), see War relief
Religion, 70; organized historical, 94-95, 96-97, 98, 103. See also Religious liberalism, liberals
"Religion of humanity," 91, 95, 96, 97, 101, 106, 107n.1
Religious education, 70, 73, 74. See also Rabbinical students
Religious freedom, 65, 67-68, 91, 92, 98. See also Church and State separation
"Religious Freedom Amendment," 100
Religious instruction, 100
Religious liberalism, liberals, 90-113

Religious observance, 9, 10, 18, 27, 37, 66, 67-68, 69-70, 72, 73, 74-75, 84, 85, 95, 100, 109n.22
Religious press, 91, 92, 93, 97, 98, 99
Religious tolerance, 65, 67, 70, 73, 98, 99, 106, 107n.2, 111n.53
RENAN, ERNEST, 93
Republican party, Republicans, 48, 49, 50, 58, 59-60
Resurrection, bodily, 94
Revolution, 37, 40. See also Russian Revolution
Revolution of 1848 (Prussian), 65
Rewards, spiritual, 94
REZNIKOFF, CHARLES, 14
RICHMAN, CLARA, see Vladeck, Clara
Riddleville, Georgia, 68
RIFKIND, JUDGE SIMON, 51, 58
Rights, equal, see Equal rights; Religious freedom
Rituals, religious, 84, 94
ROBINSON, ANNETTE, see Cohen family
Rochester (New York) Congress, National Liberal League, 101
Romania, see Rumania
ROOSEVELT, FRANKLIN DELANO, administration, 53
ROSE, MAURICE, 58
ROSENSPITZ, ALEX, 101
ROSENTHAL, HENRY, 17
Rosh Hashonah, 58
ROSS, CHARLIE, 53
ROTHSCHILD, HENRY F., 101, 111n.67
ROTHSCHILD family, 98
Roumania, see Rumania
Royal Arch Masons, 64, 70-71, 75
ROYCE, JOSIAH, 104, 113n.96
RUETHER, ROSEMARY, 110n.44
Rumania, 15, 51
Rumanian Jews, 51
RUSSELL, CHARLES EDWARD, 38
Russia, 10, 27-28, 29, 30, 31, 32, 36, 37, 40, 41n.4, 41n.14, 50, 86
Russian Christians, 98
Russian Jews, 17-28, 37, 41n.4, 86
Russian Revolution, 26, 28, 29, 30, 31, 36, 37, 40
RUTH, BABE, 9

S

Sabbath, 66, 96, 99, 100
Sabbath schools, 70. See also Sunday schools
St. Simonians, 105
Sales jobs, 81, 82
Salvation, 95, 98. See also Messiah; Truth, redemption of
"Sampson Gideon Memorial Association," 16-17
Sandersville, Georgia, 66, 69
SANKEY, IRA, 99
SARAH, 85
SAVAGE, REV. MINOT, 107n.1, 113n.99
Savannah, Georgia, 64, 68, 69, 72
SAVITCH, LEON, 36
"Sayings of the Baal-Shem-Tov," 16
SCHINDLER, RABBI SOLOMON, 107n.2, 109n.29
SCHLESINGER, RABBI MAX, 101, 110n.40, 111n.67
Scholarship, scholars, 21; religious, 90, 102, 105, 107n.2; European, 92; Protestant Bible, 94

Schools, public, see Public schools
Schools, religious, 70, 74
Science, scientific method, 91, 92, 94, 95, 96, 104, 105, 106, 107n.2
Sea Gates area, Brooklyn, New York, 15
SEAGLE, WILLIAM, 18
Second World War, 51, 52, 53, 57
Secretaries, 82
Sectarianism, religious, 92, 95, 96, 99, 102
Secularism, 100
Seligman-Hilton affair of 1877, 99
Semitic tribe, historic importance, 94
Senate, United States, 49; Immigration Committee, 17
Separation of church and state, see Church and State separation
Services, religious, see Religious observance
Settlement house movement, 34
Sewalki, Pland, 9
SHARETT, MOSHE, 58
SHAW, BERNARD, 11
"Shayne Rokhl" (pretty Rachel), 85
SHERMAN, WILLIAM TECUMSEH, 69
SHIPLACOFF, ABRAHAM I., 37
Shirtwaist makers' strike, 31-32
Shopkeepers, women, 80
Sigma Phi Sorority, 84
Silver, Abba Hillel, 59, 60
Sinai, 65
SINCLAIR, UPTON, 37
SINGER, JOSEPH, 101
SLESINGER, TESS, 20
SNETSINGER, JOHN, 50
Social activism, 40, 78, 103, 106
Social and Religious History of the Jews, 23n.14
Social change, see Modernity, Jewish women
Social Democratic Party, 29
Social duties, 70
Social injustices, 85
Socialism, socialists, 26-45, 85, 86, 89n.23, 105
Socialist Labor Party, 30
Socialist Party, 30, 31, 34, 37-38, 40
Social reform, see Social activism
Social Revolutionary Party, 27
Social work, Jewish, 81, 82, 83-84, 88n.14, 89n.21
Society, model, 97
SOLOW, HERBERT, 14, 15, 16, 20, 23n.14
SONNESCHEIN, RABBI S.H., 93, 96, 100, 107n.2
South, the (United States), 10, 64-77
Southern Jews, 10, 64-77
South Shore Temple, Chicago, Illinois, 18
Soviet Russia, 40
Soviet Union, see Union of Soviet Socialist Republics
SPINOZA, BARUCH, 98
SPIRE, ANDRE, 16
State Department, United States, 47, 49, 51, 53
Stereotypes, Jewish, 19, 112n.75, 113n.99
STERN, ELIZABETH, 86
STIMSON, HENRY, L., 54
STRAUSS, DAVID FRIEDRICH, 93
Strikes, labor, 81
STRONG, JUSTICE, 99
Students, 84, 85. See also Rabbinical students
Sudan, Africa, 50
Suez Canal Zone, 50

Sunday Blue Laws, 99, 100, 101
Sunday schools, 74. *See also* Sabbath schools.
Supernatural beliefs, 94
Supreme Court, United States, 99
Symbols, religious, 96
Synagogues, 16, 18, 19, 27, 74, 97, 98, 110n.45
Syracuse (New York) Conference, National Liberal League of America, 101, 111n.74

T

Talmudic law, 71
Talmud, 32, 71
Tammany Hall, 35
Tampa, Florida, 75
Taxation, church property, 100
TCHARNEY, DANIEL, 41n.6
Teachers, 11-12, 14, 19-20, 28, 85, 93, 94, 102
TELLER, RABBI MORRIS, 18
Temple Emanu-El, New York, New York, 110n.40
Ten lern Kreyzn, *see* Women's reading groups
TEPER, KOLYA, 36
Thanksgiving Day Proclamations, 99
Theology, theologians, 90, 91, 92, 93, 100, 105, 106, 113n.98
Third International, 40
Thomas County, Georgia, 64, 65
Thomasville, Georgia, 65, 69
TINKER, CHAUNCY, 11
Tolerance, *see* Religious tolerance
TOURO, JUDAH, 98
TOWNE, EDWARD C., 92
TOYNBEE, ARNOLD JOSEPH, 106
Trade unions, 30, 31-32, 33, 40, 78, 81, 82, 85
Traditions, religious, 91, 107n.2
Transcendentalism, 106, 107n.2
TRATTNER, RABBI EARNEST R., 18-19
Tribal Judaism, 93, 94
TRILLING, LIONEL, 12, 13-14, 16, 19, 23n.14
TROTSKY, LEON, 38
TRUMAN, HARRY S., 47, 49, 50, 51, 53-55
Truman, the Jewish Vote and Israel, 50
Truth, redemption of, 94, 95, 96, 97, 103, 104, 109n.22
Tsena Urena, 84
Tuberculosis, 79, 80
Turks, Moslem, 98

U

Udim mutsalim, 22n.1
Ukraine, 41n.4
Union of American Hebrew Congregations, 97
Union of Soviet Socialist Republics, 50
Unitarian Church, Dover, New Hampshire, 91, 108n.9
Unitarianism, Unitarians, 91, 92, 95, 105, 106, 107n.1, 107n.2, 108n.7, 110n.43, 11fn.99
United Hebrew Trades, 30, 37
United Jewish Appeal, 53, 57, 58
United Nations, 49, 58

United Order of True Sisters, 84
United States, 30, 31, 32, 35-36, 37, 38, 39, 40, 65, 74, 79, 90, 91, 92, 97, 98-100. *See also* Assimilation (Americanization); East, the; Foreign policy, United States, Immigration, United States; Military, United States; Politics, United States domestic; South, the
United Synagogue of America, 58
Unity, religious, 92, 95
Universalism, universal religion, 91, 94-97, 102, 103-104, 105-106, 107n.1, 107n.2
University of Pennsylvania, 35
Unpossessed, The, 20
UNTERMEYER, LOUIS, 18
Upper class elite, 39
"Uprising of the twenty-thousand," 31-32
"Upward mobility," Jewish immigrant women, 81, 92, 86-87
UROFSKY, MELVIN, 49
U.S.S.R., *see* Soviet Union

V

VANDENBERG, ARTHUR H. JR., 58
Vaudeville, Jewish, 17
Vichy French North Africa, 51, 52
VIESS, SHIFRA, 86
Vilna, Lithuania, 28, 29
Virginia, Jews, 98
VLADECK, BARUCH CHARNEY, 26-45; name change, 41n.3
VLADECK, CLARA (né: Richman), 34
VLADECK, MAY, 34
VLADECK, WILLIAM, 35
Vocational training, Jewish immigrant women, 82
VOLOZHIN YESHIVA, 9
Volunteer workers, 83
VOORSANGER, RABBI, 77n.42
VORSPAN, MAX, 79

W

Wages, Los Angeles, 81
WAGNER, ROBERT FERDINAND, 40
WALD, LILLIAN, 34
WARBURG, FELIX, 39
War relief, 10, 38-39, 44n.110, 57-58
Warsaw, Poland, 28, 29
WARSHOW, ROBERT, 24n.15
WASHINGTON, GEORGE, 57
Washington County, Georgia, 66
WASP eastern establishment, 49
Way Out of Agnosticism, The 104, 113n.96
WECHSLAR, JUDAH, 107n.2
WEINER, CLARA, 83
WEISGAL, MEYER, 29
Welfare system, *see* Social work, Jewish
WELLHAUSEN, JULIUS, 93
WESSSOLOWSKY, CHARLES, 64-77
WESSOLOWSKY family, 65-66; ASA, 66, 67, 68, 69; JOHANNA (né: Paiser), 68; MORRIS, 68
Westbrook, A. C., 71

White collar work, 80, 81, 82
WHITEHORN, JOSEPH, 37
White House, see Presidency, United States
White Russia, 41n.4
WILLIAMS, ROGER, 36
WINCHEFSKY, MORRIS, 31
WINKLER, RABBI MAYER, 84-85
WISE, RABBI ISAAC M., 73, 93, 96, 97, 99, 100-101, 102, 107n.1, 107n.2, 108n.12, 109n.33, 110n.37, 112n.83
WISE, RABBI STEPHEN S., 13, 54, 106, 107n.2
Wives, Jewish, 79-81, 85-86, 87
WOLFE, IDA J., 82
Women, 81, 82; Jewish immigrant, 78-89
Women's organizations, 78, 84, 89n.23
Women's rights, 85-86, 87
Worcester Free Church, Worcester, Massachusetts, 108n.7
Working class, 15, 28, 29, 31-32, 33, 85; Jewish women, 78, 79, 80-82, 86, 87
"Working man ticket," 71
Workmen's Circle, 30, 32-33, 34, 35, 85
World of Our Fathers, 32, 86
World wars, see First World War; Second World War
Worship, 70, 72, 73, 74, 100. See also Religious observance
Writers, Jewish, 8-25, 85
WROTTENBERG, JEANETTE, 83-84

Y

Yaddo, 14
"Yahudim," 39
Yale University, 11-12, 19-20, 23n.8
YEZIERSKA, ANZIA, 86
Yiddish culture, 28, 29, 33, 37, 85
Yiddishkayt, 85. See also Yiddish culture
Yiddish language, 15, 16, 17-18, 30, 31, 34, 84, 85
Yiddish literature, 9, 15, 29, 30, 36-37, 41n.6
Yiddish press, 9, 26, 30, 78, 85
Yiddish-speaking literati, 13
"Yiden un di gantzkayt fun der mishpokhe" ("Jews and family solidarity"), 85
Young Women's Hebrew Association, 84

Z

ZANGWILL, LOUIS, 16
Zikhroynes fun a Bialystoker froy, 80
Zimmerman Note, 38
Zionism, Zionists, 9, 10, 15, 28, 39, 47, 49, 50, 57
Zionist Organization of America, 15, 49
Zionist-socialists, 85
Zunland, 85